MIRRORS

— OF —

JESUS

A MEMOIR

I hope the light of Christ
fills your life and heart.

Michelle Dennis
Echristenen

MIRRORS

—— OF ——

JESUS

A Memoir

FINDING PARALLELS
OF CHRIST IN OUR LIVES

MICHELLE DENNIS CHRISTENSEN

CFI
AN IMPRINT OF CEDAR FORT, INC.
SPRINGVILLE, UTAH

Editor's note: All Bible references refer to the King James Version (KJV) unless otherwise noted.

ISBN 13: 978-1-4621-4454-9

Published by CFI, an imprint of Cedar Fort, Inc.
2373 W. 700 S., Suite 100, Springville, UT 84663
Distributed by Cedar Fort, Inc., www.cedarfort.com

Library of Congress Control Number: 2022947371

Cover design by Courtney Proby
Cover design © 2023 Cedar Fort, Inc.
Edited by Katie Lewis

Printed in the United States of America

10 9 8 7 6 5 4 3 2 1

Printed on acid-free paper

DEDICATION

To my husband, Martin

Of all the love stories ever told,
ours is my favorite.

ACKNOWLEDGMENTS

I owe my deepest and greatest thanks to my dear husband, Martin. This book opens your life to others, and rather than shrinking away from it, you always encouraged me to move forward. Thank you for crying with me as both of us relived moments both terrifying and tender. Thank you for listening when I read every chapter to you. You helped me fix a messy first draft and wordsmith the final draft. You really should be listed as a coauthor. I love you!

I also want to thank each of my children, William, Adam, Katie, Brian, Nicole, and Dennis. This book makes you vulnerable, too. I'm grateful for your willingness to let me share part of your story, without which this book wouldn't be complete.

Thank you to my family and to Martin's family. Our parents, Peyton and Denice Dennis and Don and Arda Jean Christensen, were our rocks and support during this time. Our siblings, their spouses, and many other family members volunteered, served, loved, and strengthened us during our time of trial. I'm so grateful for forever families.

To all those who came to our aid—ward members, visiting teachers, neighbors, and friends—we are forever indebted to you. You fed our family, cleaned our house, weeded our yard, shoveled our snow. You drove Martin to the hospital for blood tests. You sat with our children at church. You loved us, wept with us, fasted and prayed for us, and bore witness of God's power and mercy through your words and actions.

I cannot forget the Intermountain Transplant team, the many doctors, nurses, and medical professionals who helped us through dialysis, transplant, and recovery. Their love, care, concern, skill, and expertise made all the difference.

To my writing community, I owe my heartfelt thanks. Without you, this book never would have been written. My summer critique group, Rebecca Hicken, Allison Bundy, and Michelle Henrie, worked through more than eight rewrites of my first chapter as they helped me discover my voice and story-telling structure. Michelle Wilson gave valuable feedback early in the process. My ANWA critique group, including Mindy Strunk, Laura Rollins, Amanda Jones, Jenelle Allred and others cheered me on when I was stuck. My beta readers, Tara Allred-Niekamp, Allison Bundy, Jenelle Allred, and Kim Dennis provided vast feedback and insight. They helped me change my first chapter—again, brainstormed revisions for the section when both Martin and I were in surgery, and pointed out the good spots as well as the rough bits I needed to change.

To everyone at Cedar Fort Publishing, thank you. Angela Johnson took a chance on me as a first-time author. Courtney Proby designed a cover that surpassed my dreams and brought the focus of this book onto the Savior, which is where it should be. Katie Lewis worked hard to edit, format, typeset, and make the inside look beautiful. Heather Holm made communication easy. Thank you, also, to the rest of the Cedar Fort team who worked behind the scenes.

Finally, and most important, I wish to thank my Heavenly Father and Savior, Jesus Christ. I love Them. This book is my humble attempt to testify of Their goodness, love, and mercy in my life.

CONTENTS

Contents

CHAPTER 1

FINDING MIRRORS OF CHRIST IN OUR LIVES

"All things bear record of [God]."

(Moses 6:63)

The truth was sobering. Without a great sacrifice, Martin would die.

We'd been at the hospital the entire day meeting with doctors, social workers, nutritionists, and more, hoping Martin would qualify for a kidney transplant. The sheer volume of information, along with intense emotions, was a lot to take in. The thirty-minute ride allowed us the opportunity to discuss it before greeting the chaos of a family we'd left unattended.

"What do you think?" I asked Martin on the way home.

Martin let out a heavy sigh as we contemplated the future.

His daily life was miserable on hemodialysis, a treatment meant to keep you alive but not make you healthy. People on this form of dialysis die in an average of three years (Stokes). If something didn't change, my fifty-one-year-old husband would pass away as a young man. Of our six children, we still had three living at home, the youngest just out of second grade. Martin needed to live.

Yet, in order for him to live, someone had to make an enormous sacrifice. Martin could receive a kidney from a deceased donor once a suitable match was found. For that to happen, the grieving family of an individual who just died or who lived on life-support, would have to make the tough, time-sensitive decision to donate the organs before the organs lost viability ("Donation After Life").

If Martin received a kidney from a living donor, that person would have to undergo major surgery, one more difficult than many other procedures. With advanced technology, most surgeries were outpatient or required only one to two days in the hospital. Not a transplant. The donor might stay in the hospital up to a week. Plus, any surgery was risky, especially major surgery, and while the probability was low, it still existed that someone could die during the operation.

"It's humbling," Martin said. "Today it hit me just what we're asking another individual to do. Just for me."

How could he ask that of someone?

As we talked, I saw a strong parallel to our Savior. Just as someone had to sacrifice to save Martin, the Savior sacrificed to save all of us. Without His atonement, we would die physically, spiritually, eternally. The more I contemplated the sacrifice required to save Martin, the better I understood the Savior's gift for me, for Martin, and for every individual who ever lived.

The scriptures teach that "all things bear record of him," (Moses 6:63), but I never expected this type of similarity, the need for someone to offer such an intense personal gift for Martin to live. How had it come to this? We'd only been married such a short time, less time than I had spent as a single adult.

Like many teenage girls who are members of The Church of Jesus Christ of Latter-day Saints, my future dreams had centered on getting married and raising a family. At Ricks College, I trained to be a secretary, so it would prepare me with a skill to put a husband through college. Much to my surprise, I received my associate's degree still single. With a marketable skill, I got a job, positive I would find the perfect man and soon begin raising a family. It didn't happen.

One night when I was in my early twenties, I had a dream, the essence of which stayed vivid over the years, even though the details remained shadowed. I dreamt I was engaged to marry a large man whose strong arms enveloped me in a secure embrace. My love for him outshone anything I'd felt for previous flames.

I awoke knowing the Lord had given me hope I would marry. Year after year passed, and I clung to that memory. Though I dated a lot, nothing ever worked out. As the years advanced, the memory of the dream lingered in the back of my mind. However, I didn't know if the Lord meant to fulfill that blessing in this life or the next.

I prayed for strength and perspective. "Heavenly Father, please help me accept Thy will. Help me be content."

With faith in God, I threw myself into alternate plans. I returned to school and completed a master's degree in my early thirties. The Lord helped me build a wonderful, rewarding life, complete with an exhilarating career and opportunities for service in the Church.

In one of my callings, I served in the Young Women's organization with two individuals who also volunteered in the Scouting program. They were on the staff of a week-long leadership training for adults called Wood Badge, and they recruited me to attend. Why not? It would be fun camping for a week, and the classes would benefit my job. Yet an unsettling but exciting impression lurked in the shadows, nagging, insisting on a different purpose for attending. It informed me I'd meet someone.

I dismissed the thought because those elusive feelings had been wrong more times than I could count. Besides, that would be impossible in a camp full of married Scoutmasters. Right? My life was good, and I didn't want my hopes dashed. Again.

In August, I left the world behind for eight days in the Uinta Mountains in northern Utah. On the opening day, rain dripped onto my hair from the overhanging pine tree branches. The cold, damp air chilled my enthusiasm and heightened my nerves. What on earth was I doing up there? I knew nothing about Scouting. I spied my new team, one woman, one teenager, and three married Scoutmasters. They were talking with our team leader. The cold mountain air pierced my flimsy rain poncho, and I shivered as I moved across the wet mountain grass to join them.

I tilted my head up to look at the six-foot-six team leader. His name tag read, "Martin." I knew that name.

He was the staff member one of the Young Women's advisors had referred to several months earlier when she gave a lesson about rising above our trials. She'd met a man at a leadership camp. His humor, compassion, and enthusiasm had helped their team become a cohesive group. She'd thought he had it all, the perfect life. The night before they left, she discovered the opposite. Six months earlier, his wife had died from breast cancer.

When she told the story, I'd pictured a sweet older man helping others, and it warmed my heart.

There he stood. My team leader. And he wasn't even close to seventy years old.

I smiled at him, and a feeling settled in my stomach—not just a feeling, but that feeling, the very feeling I'd hoped for but given up on years earlier. The feeling that this man might end up being more than my team leader. It excited and frightened me. I moved forward with cautious optimism.

During the week, I hardly took my gaze off his deep-set blue eyes when he presented the leadership lessons. At an impromptu astronomy lesson he taught, I stood next to him while he pointed out different constellations in the dark, cold mountain sky. I'm sure my eyes shone brighter than the millions of stars twinkling down upon us as I tried to catch his attention.

When it rained and Martin saw how my cheap poncho didn't keep me dry, he brought me a better one to use. I thanked him, and he waved it aside, saying he'd do that for any of our team. The expression in his eyes, though, communicated something different. We were connecting on a deeper level.

Our conversations around the campfires seemed private, even though the entire team was present. Every discussion we had, from favorite books to quantum mechanics, deepened my interest. As he talked about his four children, ages eleven down to three, his love for them was clear and impressed me.

Every quality I had ever wanted he appeared to possess, including my frivolous desire to marry a very tall man. Each day I became more and more attracted to him. I treasured each moment of the enchanted bubble we lived in, away from the pressures of normal existence.

The week ended too soon. Real life and real-life problems beckoned us back. Anxious uncertainty filled my heart the last few hours before I left. I didn't want to drive down the mountain and abandon the romantic magic. Would it die once we got home, crushed under the weight of reality, everyday routines, and pressures so distant from the charmed days in the mountains?

Not if I could help it. I wanted the opportunity for a relationship to develop out of the spark that had ignited during the week. If the tiny flame got doused, then I'd move on. But I wasn't about to let the flame die without adding fuel first.

"I'd like to meet your kids," I said before I left.

Martin returned a cautious smile, but I watched his eyes follow me as I walked to the car that was my ride home. I smiled and waved goodbye.

The following week, before I could make good on my plans to deliver him a fresh peach pie, he called me. We talked on the phone for five hours. We talked again the next day and went on a date the following Saturday. Our relationship progressed quickly, and we got married three months later.

My dream from years ago, the shadowed hint of a promise from Heavenly Father, had come true in very literal ways. Martin was a large man who wrapped me in security every time he held me. My love for him surpassed anything I'd ever experienced before.

Now, after only fourteen years of marriage, we faced the possibility of his premature death.

The weight of this trial would have crushed me without the help of Jesus Christ. I needed Him, I searched for Him, and one way I found Him was by looking at how my life's experiences mirrored His.

Knowing Jesus pled for another way when He was in Gethsemane gave me courage to face the trials I didn't want to face. Knowing Jesus wept with Martha reassured me He would succor me. Knowing Jesus sacrificed himself so we could live gave me faith as we searched for a donor so that Martin could live.

The scriptures tell us that all things from God typify Jesus Christ (see 2 Nephi 11:4). I believe when it says "all things," it means all things, including our own lives. Mirrors of Jesus surround us and are unique to each individual's life and experiences. Many are obvious.

Some are not. When we search for and discover the mirrors in our lives, we grow to trust Jesus Christ more.

I needed that kind of trust when the doctors diagnosed Martin with kidney failure, and I faced the most difficult trial of my life.

CHAPTER 2

JESUS SPEAKS THROUGH PROPHETS

"Surely the Lord God will do nothing, but he revealeth his secret unto his servants the prophets."

(Amos 3:7)

As a girl, I loved thick foggy days in the middle of winter. During elementary school recess, I'd make my way to the very back of the expansive field. The fog obscured the building, the playgrounds, and the teacher on duty. In my imagination, the mists swallowed me whole, and I wandered in the wilderness in search of human life.

It was a fun game to be lost on the school field, but it's not such a fun game when you're really lost, especially on a dark night in a strange town. It's even worse when you're lost symbolically. You can feel as if overnight you're not strolling through your familiar life anymore. You might wonder: When did this hostile environment overtake me? How did I get here? I never saw it coming. I have no idea how to escape from this desolate place. What on earth do I do now?

That's where we found ourselves thirteen and a half years after we were married. Like Lehi, we traveled "in a dark and dreary waste" (1 Nephi 8:7). Lehi's Arabian-type desert wilderness encompassed me. Sand blew every direction, obscured the view, buried the path, and hid the light. I had no idea what to do.

Martin's health had declined for no obvious reason. At his age, a man in his late forties, he should have strength and energy, and it perplexed us because he didn't. However, his health had declined at such a slow pace we didn't pay attention as it occurred. All we understood is that he lived with fatigue.

Bit by bit the weariness grew worse and interfered with his work. Martin managed several duplexes we own, which provided our only source of income. At first, he skipped work a day here and a day there, and he didn't respond to the renters' requests immediately. The exhaustion grew stronger, and his ability to repair, restore, and re-rent units worsened.

He visited a urologist about an infection, and the doctor put him on antibiotics. After two weeks, the infection returned. The doctor switched medications and put him on a sulfa drug for two months. Although the infection cleared, the sulfa drugs left him with GI tract problems. At a follow-up appointment, the doctor declared Martin better.

Except he wasn't.

A couple of years later, he saw another doctor for acid reflux and related problems. The doctor performed a colonoscopy and an endoscopy before he pronounced Martin fine. Nothing wrong. He wrote a prescription for acid reflux. "That should help."

Except it didn't.

Years passed, and Martin's health worsened. Migraines plagued him with increasing intensity and frequency. His thoughts grew foggy and confused, making it hard for him to concentrate. Fatigue sapped his strength and made it impossible for him to accomplish simple tasks that required little effort when he was well. Despite the weariness, his sleep was fitful and never restored his energy.

"You should go see a doctor," I said once.

"Tell me who to go to, and I'll go." Frustration laced his voice.

"I don't know." I grimaced.

"Yeah. That's the problem. I've already been to two different doctors, and all they tell me is that I'm fine. I'm not fine, but they can't find anything wrong."

Not knowing how to answer, I let the issue drop.

Martin's condition degenerated, vacancies increased, and our finances plummeted.

Life was so heavy. Discouragement pulled me down day after day, and the whirling mists and sand around me obscured any view, any hope. How would we ever get out of this situation? Bills beckoned to be paid. Missionary sons needed financial support. College approached for our older children with no means of helping them. There was no money.

Worry walked with me every waking moment as I pushed one foot in front of the other in the blinding storm. I would drag my body through the morning chores, get breakfast for the kids, clean the house, and exercise—or feel guilty for not exercising (although I couldn't because I had zero energy).

Many mornings after the last child departed for school, I knelt and pled with God for comfort, for help, for guidance. I let the tears flow as I explained, in great detail, the sorrows of my heart. At the end of the prayers, I wouldn't feel much change, so I'd get off my knees and continue with my tasks.

By mid-morning, peace would fill my thoughts and actions. When had that happened? When had my frame of mind switched from darkness to light? I couldn't pinpoint it. It just happened. The problems still existed, but God wrapped me in the comfort of His love and encouragement, which gave me strength to continue.

Every time I repeated the process and opened up myself to receive help from the Lord, it worked. When I prayed for strength through the power of Christ's atonement, then stood and went about my day, a change happened. And I never could identify the exact moment it occurred. Long-term solutions were not suddenly and distinctly poured into my head with a clear road map of what to do next. The fog, sand, and mists did not disappear. No. The problems still existed, but God helped me get through the next few days, or hours, or even minutes.

Everyone experiences the sustaining power of God differently. Praying like this might work for you. It might not. Your way of finding relief might come from listening to uplifting music, serving others, exercising. Regardless of the methods, the prophets and

Church leaders have promised us that God is always ready to give us immediate help—if we turn to Him and allow His help—even while we wait for long-term solutions to difficult problems.

Elder Kyle S. McKay, a member of the Seventy, reassured us when he said, "the immediate goodness of God comes to all who call upon Him with real intent and full purpose of heart. This includes those who cry out in earnest desperation, when deliverance seems so distant and suffering seems prolonged, even intensified" ("The Immediate Goodness of God," 105).

Though the Lord sustained us, Martin's health didn't recover. The wilderness sandstorms raged for several years. He didn't know what to do, and I didn't know what to do. Every single day he battled for his health. On bad days, he stayed in bed all day trying to recuperate. On semi-bad days, he took painkillers and hauled himself off to work, determined to push through the exhaustion, the headaches, the brain fog.

Over time, Martin got the empty units ready to rent. He ignored physical pain and fatigue to install sprinkler systems, repair holes in walls, and replace broken appliances. When the kids were in school, I spent hours painting one unit and then another. Our two older sons, both in their early twenties, helped their dad between work and their college classes. The younger four kids also contributed by painting, cleaning, and mowing lawns. After several grueling months, we filled every unit.

Now, at long last, Martin had time to heal without responsibilities interfering. Or so I thought. Instead, less than a month after full occupancy, a renter called with a problem.

I had been running errands one freezing February afternoon in 2011. Cold followed me into the house when I arrived home, so I hurried to shut the winter weather outside. Turning around, I saw Martin on the couch with his legs resting on a pillow on the sofa arm, his feet dangling over the end.

My shoulders dropped. What was he doing home? I thought he'd be at the duplexes taking care of a renter's maintenance problem. She'd called a few days earlier, but Martin had been too sick to respond right away. He'd planned to go that day.

"I'm sorry, but I couldn't go," he said. "I threw up. I'll try again, tomorrow."

Both disappointed and concerned, I crossed the room and gave him a hug. Cold from outside seemed to push through the door to penetrate my heart. Although I tried not to show it, my insides tightened, and the knots in my stomach joined those in my shoulders and neck. Gloom enshrouded me.

How could we afford to lose another renter? If Martin didn't get the maintenance done promptly, the resident would be angry. Then what? Frustrated tenants left as soon as their leases were up. We knew that too well.

We did not know what to do. I detected no hint of light in front, to the sides, or in back of me. Darkness covered my path, and each second loomed heavy with worry and frustration.

Something had to be done. I contemplated the alternatives, and the lump in my stomach grew. The repairs were beyond my skill level. Hiring a contractor was out of the question because they were so expensive.

Martin continued. "I have a massive headache, worse than normal. I think I have a sinus infection."

Desperate, I stared at my sick husband and grappled for something—anything—to help. "You need to see a doctor. At least for the sinus infection."

"All right. But who?"

"InstaCare? Or, Dr. Stevens, my parents' doctor? They like him."

Martin agreed, and I scheduled an appointment with Dr. Stevens. A couple of days later, we sat in his office. Martin recited the problems that plagued him, both the current sinus infection and the mysteries he had dealt with for years.

"When was your last physical and blood workup?" Dr. Stevens asked.

"I don't know. Not for a long time. Years."

"Let's get this infection cleared up first and then come back for a well-care visit."

We departed with a follow-up appointment and a prescription for an antibiotic. The antibiotic worked right away, and Martin found immense relief. Maybe, just maybe, this doctor would help. I wanted to believe, but doubted.

I didn't recognize it then, but the darkness did not have complete reign. God was present, even though I couldn't see Him through the swirling mess in front of me. He knew the details and the solution. He knew that if we did not address the real problem—the one hidden deep—Martin would die early. He knew Martin had to visit a doctor to get pointed in the right direction, to show us the way.

However, given Martin's past failures with doctors, that would not happen unless he had a compelling reason. A sinus infection was compelling; it was something we believed a doctor could help with. God could have healed Martin's infection through the prayer of faith. In His wisdom, though, He didn't. He let the infection direct us toward the help we needed.

Once the infection cleared, we met with the doctor for the routine exam. After the physical, he ordered standard blood tests to gain some clues about Martin's long-term problems, and we scheduled a follow-up appointment for the next week to discuss the lab results.

As we waited, we wondered. Would the labs reveal something wasn't right? If they did, what could be the problem? What if they showed nothing amiss? What then? Martin still felt awful; what would we do? On the other hand, what if something was terribly wrong? Then what? Wouldn't it be better to have the tests return as normal? Around and around our thoughts went.

Martin registered for a patient portal that contained the results, and we took an early peek. They showed his creatinine was super high, over thirteen where normal was one or less. A number so high above normal meant bad news. But what kind of bad news? What did it mean? For that matter, what on earth was creatinine? Google said it had something to do with kidneys. But what? Unable to decipher the numbers ourselves, we had to wait for his next appointment.

"Oh, that can't be right." Dr. Stevens said as soon as he saw Martin's off-the-chart number. "It has to be a lab error because if the number was right, you wouldn't be here in my office but in the hospital on dialysis."

Dialysis? What was that? I had a vague memory of a neighbor who had been on dialysis. He died. That didn't sound good. As my fears mounted, the doctor reassured me.

"It's probably just a false reading. Let's test it again, and see what it says. But," he said, "I'm concerned about this." He circled the figure by the letters PSA, which stand for prostate-specific antigen and is an early warning of prostate cancer. "This reads six point zero one. Normal is less than four."

Eyes wide, I stared at him.

The doctor continued in a calm, practical voice. "There are several possible explanations for a high PSA count. Yes, one is cancer. But that's not the only reason it could be high. And at your age," he looked at Martin, "it's probably not cancer."

His words relieved me, and it made sense, too. Prostate cancer hits older men most of the time, and Martin had just turned fifty-one six weeks earlier.

"Still, it's important to get it checked. Just in case." The doctor's voice was firm. "Find a urologist and schedule an appointment right away. Sometimes you have to wait a few weeks before you can see one."

"What about his kidney function?" I asked, focused once again on the troubling number. "Could the urologist help?"

"No. He needs a kidney doctor for that. But like I said, don't worry. We'll retest it. I'm sure it's an anomaly. The most important thing to do is get the prostate checked as soon as possible."

With a new lab order in hand, we stopped at the clinic for a blood draw before going home. Then I called and scheduled an appointment with a specialist that Martin's family members had used.

"Sure," the receptionist said. "We have an opening tomorrow? Would that work?"

Would that work? Of course. I couldn't believe it. They had an opening the next day. For a new patient. When does that happen?

Martin and I both thanked God for a small miracle.

Before we met with Dr. Stevens, we had no clue where we needed to go or even how to find out where to go. Because he had more knowledge and experience, he recognized what Martin needed to do. He pointed us in the right direction to get help.

The doctor's role mirrored the way the Lord guides His children. Jesus Christ gives us direction through his prophets. "Surely the Lord God will do nothing, but he revealeth his secret unto his servants the prophets" (Amos 3:7).

I love the Primary song, "Follow the Prophet." Six times the simple chorus repeats the counsel "follow the prophet." It concludes with the phrase, "He knows the way" (*Children's Songbook*, 110). President Russell M. Nelson said, "Ordained Apostles of Jesus Christ always testify of Him. They point the way as we make our way through the heart-wrenching maze of our mortal experiences" ("Hear Him," 90). When blowing sands obliterate the light, we can heed the words of the prophets because they can see what we cannot.

Yet even when we are trying to follow the prophets, sometimes we face bleak darkness before the light appears. The night before his appointment, Martin battled extreme darkness and fear.

CHAPTER 3

CHRIST IS THE MASTER HEALER

"Return unto me, and repent of your sins . . . that I may heal you."

(3 Nephi 9:13)

When our youngest son, Dennis, was four years old, trains fascinated him. Martin would help him build an elaborate route using toy tracks. Around and around, the battery-powered Thomas the Tank Engine pulled freight cars, passenger cars, and a caboose. One small switch on the track would send Thomas zipping down a different, dangerous path with a sharp curve. Giggles filled the air when the train capsized. Small, chubby hands righted each piece, fixed the switch, and sent the procession on its way.

One small switch. That's all it took to derail an entire train.

One small switch sent Martin down a trajectory that threatened his life before we figured out we were on the wrong track. The fatigue and other signs started out so small, we ignored them. As his health worsened, he tried seeking help. No success. Discouragement and futility kept him on the current path. Martin's health declined to a dangerous point. One small decision that never got corrected landed him so far away from where we wanted to be. The night before his appointment with the specialist, the consequences were vivid.

I plodded downstairs to get some washing done. Balancing the laundry basket with one arm, I flipped on the light with the other and stopped at the doorway. Water covered the cement floor. What had happened? Didn't we have enough to deal with?

I fought back the tears and stepped into a big puddle in the unfinished room. Sounds of spraying and draining water drew my attention to the water heater where I found the answer. Water was pouring out of the bottom.

My head dropped. Not now. Not with Martin so ill. We had to have hot water, especially during the chilly March weather. A quick glance around the room revealed no water damage to the storage boxes, since they rested on a two-inch platform. At least a new drain drew off enough water to prevent other damage.

With heavy steps, I found the main water line and turned it off before I trudged up the stairs to find my husband.

"Martin?" I said. My voice caught.

He looked at me from where he rested on the couch.

"I'm sorry, but the water heater went out. I think the bottom has rusted through."

"Can't we get a break?" he said. With a groan, he struggled to a sitting position.

"I know." I put my arms around him and shook my head. "I know."

Martin stood and shuffled through the house to get his keys and wallet.

My heart ached when I saw how the simplest movement taxed his abilities. This was the man who used to toss a bale of hay onto a wagon with only one arm, while other men struggled to do it using both. This was the man whose massive strength hoisted an entire beam up a ladder alone when he built houses in the nineties. This was the man who now struggled to walk to the car.

Darkness cloaked our spirits, along with the evening sky. Brian, our seventeen-year-old son, helped Martin pull the extra seats out of the silver Honda Odyssey van to make room for a new water heater from Home Depot.

As soon as they left, I wrestled with storage boxes to clear a path. The minutes dragged on. I set about making dinner—without water. At the sound of the opening garage door echoing in my house, I darted outside, worried about Martin.

Father and son tugged the heavy tank out of the van, balanced it on a hand truck, and bumped it one step at time down the stairwell. Martin panted and needed to rest before continuing. Sweat pooled on his forehead head as he wrestled with the bulky contraption. His hands shook when he unscrewed the pipes to the old tank, and his breath came in quick gasps when he hooked up the fresh water supply. His limbs grew shakier by the minute and looked like they'd fail him when he pushed and prodded the water heater into place.

Young and inexperienced, Brian helped where he could, but his lack of expertise left the bulk of the burden on Martin.

Four anxious hours later, I turned on the tap to the main water line. Gushing water echoed inside the metal tank. Martin lit the gas pilot light and adjusted the temperature knob so it could heat fifty gallons of cold water.

He stumbled upstairs and collapsed on the bed. Fatigue held him prisoner, and the strain to lift his arms and legs to remove his shirt and pants depleted any reserves he had left. Between short periods of rest, he undressed and got ready for bed, where he dropped once again and lay motionless with no ability to lift his head or roll over.

Once the younger kids were in bed, I curled up next to my spent husband. He wrapped a limp arm around me while his chest quivered against my body. His rapid heart rate pounded and thumped in my ears.

"Michelle," he said after a few minutes of silence, broken only by his strenuous breathing.

His tone was so quiet yet so intense that I had to lift my head a fraction to hear him.

"If something happens . . . to me . . . if I don't get better . . . you'll be okay. We have the . . . duplexes."

"Martin? What?" I pushed onto one arm to look at him. Fatigue lined his face. Sweat rested on his forehead. His breath escaped in halting gasps.

"Just know, you'll be okay. Financially, I mean. We have the duplexes."

Silence. The hum of the furnace started. A creak reverberated deep in the house. Then more silence.

"I want you to know how much I love you," he said at last. His voice was quiet and forced.

"I love you, too. But . . ." My voice trailed off. I lay back down on the bed against him.

"The kids. Make sure they know I love them, too. They need to know that."

"They do. But, Martin? It's going to be okay. The Lord answered our prayers, and you have an appointment to see Dr. Kinder tomorrow. It'll be okay. You'll get better.

"I . . . I'm . . . I'm really sick. I don't know if I'll ever get better. It doesn't seem like the doctors can help. If I don't get better, you'll be okay. It's important to me you know that."

"You'll get better. You will. This is just the fatigue and stress and worry talking," I said, hoping to convince myself as well as him. I pressed my body tighter against his.

Worry crept from my stomach to my heart and tightened my shoulders and neck. Later that night, I buried my head in my pillow and hid ragged, unsteady breaths from my husband. How had we followed the track that led us through such dangerous perils? This couldn't be happening. I prayed the doctor could help put us back on the right course before Martin's train derailed.

I needed him. Our family needed him. We had three children still at home, two in elementary school and one in high school. Only one of our three young adults had married, and all six relied on him for strength, wisdom, and support. Martin had to be around for them to grow up, graduate, go on missions, marry. He had to get better. I couldn't do it alone.

Maybe the next day would give us some answers. After all, a miracle occurred when we got the appointment so soon. That had to mean something. Didn't it? I prayed with my whole soul for strength and guidance.

Not getting medical help for several years before we met with Dr. Stevens was not a sin. Nevertheless, it was a mistake with grave, unintended consequences. It was a mistake that plunged our family into darkness. It was a mistake that we couldn't fix on our own. After many years, Martin sought medical help. He turned to a doctor, to a person who could help him heal, help him recover.

Our mistakes in life, whether they are unintentional or willful acts of rebellion, can have grave consequences, just like turning one small switch on a railroad. They can plunge us into darkness along a foreign track and can lead to serious complications. Just as we needed to turn to a healer to help Martin, we must turn to the Master Healer in our lives. Christ's invitation to the Nephites is also an invitation to us, "Will ye not now return unto me, and repent of your sins, and be converted, that I may heal you?" (3 Nephi 9:13).

It's simple. President Russell M. Nelson said, "How can we be healed by Him? We can more fully repent" ("Jesus Christ—The Master Healer," 86). Even if our mistakes are unintentional, they propel us down paths that need a course correction. Christ always extends the invitation. Over and over, he says, "Come unto me" (3 Nephi 9:14; Mormon 3:2; Matthew 11:28). When we seek help from one who is qualified to help, from Jesus Christ, we turn our lives around and in the process return to Him.

Martin sought help from one qualified as well. At our appointment the next day, Dr. Kinder walked into the room and shook our hands.

"Tell me what's going on," he said to Martin. The doctor put on reading glasses and glanced at the lab results.

We drew his attention to the bad kidney measurement.

"Don't worry about that number," he said with a wave. "That's got to be a lab error."

"That's what Dr. Stevens said, so he had it retested," I said. Dr. Kinder couldn't miss this. It was too important. "The results came back yesterday afternoon, and the creatinine measured over eleven the second time."

Stunned, Dr. Kinder shook his head. "That's not good. You need to see a nephrologist."

"A what?" Martin and I said at the same time.

"Nephrologist. A kidney specialist. They're the people who can help you in that area." His attention returned to the labs. "Your PSA count? That's my area of expertise. A high number doesn't always mean cancer. Let's check it out."

He found no signs of prostate cancer and figured an enlarged prostate caused the high PSA number. He told us about a procedure he could perform that should help and asked us to stop by the scheduler's desk on the way out to arrange it. With that, he started toward the door.

Relief flooded me from top to bottom. We had avoided cancer. Kidney problems didn't seem as ominous.

"Before you leave," Martin said, halting Dr. Kinder's exit. "Will you feel this?" Martin lay back on the examination table and pushed a section on his stomach. "To me it seems hard where it shouldn't be hard. Something's not right."

With the expert hands of an experienced physician, the doctor poked and prodded. He looked at Martin. Concern showed in his eyes.

"You're right," he said. "Something's wrong. There's a big mass there. A tumor or something. We need to get it checked immediately."

A tumor? Cancer? The words bounced around my brain. I looked at Martin in fear and saw his eyes reflect the same emotion. He knew about the devastating prognosis of stomach cancer because his grandfather had died from it.

"Come with me," the doctor said, taking charge when we couldn't think. He took time out of his busy schedule and escorted us through turning corridors to the surgery scheduler where he could impress upon her his urgent request.

"I need a CT scan for Martin. Today," he said in a firm, authoritative voice. "Call around until you find a place that can take him. As soon as possible."

As the scheduler picked up the phone, he turned to us.

"When you get the scans, come back here. Today, if you can. Bring the images with you." He paused, looked at us, and must have noticed my rigid body and taut face. He put a hand on Martin's shoulder and continued in a softer tone. "Don't worry. We'll figure it out. We'll take care of you."

Another miracle occurred when the scheduler found a facility with an open CT machine less than two miles away. They had an open spot in an hour.

Sixty minutes later, we entered the waiting room. St. Patrick's Day decorations adorned the reception area and the walls around the room. The nurses and front-desk staff wore varying shades and quantities of green. The cheerful area and their friendly manners stood in stark contrast to the heavy, dark cloud that hovered over me. My luck had run out; there'd be no pot of gold for me.

Martin moved to the back, plopped into a dark arm chair, and pulled out his phone.

"I want to update the kids," he said. He believed in open communication with his children, and even though we didn't have a firm diagnosis, he felt like they should know.

"Adam," he said after our married son answered the phone. "I'm calling with an update. I'm waiting to get a CT scan, but I want you to know it doesn't look good. They found a mass in my abdomen, maybe a tumor. I might have cancer." Martin's voice cracked.

I couldn't imagine how hard this must be for Adam. My four older children had already lost one parent to the dreaded disease. That wasn't all. A close relative of ours was losing a battle with liver cancer. They had seen too much cancer in their lives.

"I want you to know, I love you. I'll keep you posted. Good bye." Quiet terror made his voice soft. He repeated the conversation two more times as he contacted our adult children. He'd have the tough conversation with the three younger kids after they got home from school.

"I love you, so much. You make me proud," he said every time.

Thirty heart-breaking minutes later, the technician took him back. I waited and tried to focus on something other than worry and fear. After half an hour lapsed, Martin plodded back to the sitting area and dropped onto the chair next to me while we waited for copies of the scans. Questions loomed with no answers, or answers that remained concealed in the large manila envelope the nurse handed us a short time later.

With dread still heavy, we returned to the urology clinic. A staff member escorted us to a small procedure room. Anxiety filled the small space where we awaited the verdict. Second after second, minute after minute, passed in silence.

Dr. Kinder entered, a puzzling, gigantic smile plastered across his face. "This is good news," he said.

We stared at him.

"Didn't they tell you what they found?"

"No."

"It's not a tumor. That hard mass? It's your bladder," he said with a laugh. "I can't believe it. I've never seen anything like it."

He pushed the scans into the metal clip and turned on a light to shine through the images. Cross section after cross section of Martin's abdominal cavity appeared.

"Look. There's your bladder, and that spot right there is where it should be. Your bladder, though, is holding so much fluid that it's way up there." He pointed to a position high in the abdomen. "It's crowding all your other organs. No wonder you don't feel well. I'll bet the urine has refluxed into the kidneys, and that's what's causing your kidneys to fail."

He turned to look at us.

"We need to drain it, take the pressure off your kidneys. That should help you begin to feel better. I'll do that now."

I smiled and gripped Martin's hands. Hope lightened the room. Martin wouldn't die of stomach cancer, and it looked like he'd get better.

Months of neglect, although unintentional, had wreaked havoc. It took finding a physician who knew what to look for so Martin's healing journey could begin. If we ignore slight course corrections and continue on the current track, we often have to suffer through enormous problems that require extensive help in order for them to heal. Like the small switch in a train station, a small decision can take us more than a thousand miles off course before we identify or acknowledge the problem and then take the lengthy measures to correct it. The earlier we turn to the Master Healer, the easier it will be to repent and let Him make us whole.

As easy as that is to say, applying it might not be. Just as we didn't know the true source of Martin's declining health, we might not always know when we're off the right course, not know what's wrong in our lives. To help us find the answers, Elder Larry Lawrence of the Seventy counseled, "Humbly ask the Lord the following question: 'What is keeping me from progressing?' In other words: 'What lack I yet?' Then wait quietly for a response" ("What Lack I Yet?," 35).

Perhaps you, like me, are afraid of asking that type of question. I already know that I fall short in so many areas. The list is way too long and way too overwhelming. I'm afraid the answers would derail me.

Elder Lawrence recognized the tendency to become paralyzed with a lengthy list of imperfections. He said, "The Holy Ghost doesn't tell us to improve everything at once. If He did, we would become discouraged and give up. The Spirit works with us at our own speed, one step at a time" ("What Lack I Yet?," 34).

Bit by bit, through slight course corrections, we can stay close to our Redeemer, making minor alterations daily that keep us going the right direction. More complex problems will take more time to bring us back on track, but it doesn't matter to the Savior, who always has his hand extended out to us. We need to remember patience and persistence. Elder Neil L. Andersen said, "For most, repentance is more of a journey than a one-time event. It is not easy. To change is difficult" ("Repent," 41).

This was true for Martin's health. Even though we had light and hope, his condition was so far off course that the way back would be slow, arduous, and awash with the unknown.

CHAPTER 4

SUFFERING TEACHES US

*"Though he were a Son, yet learned he obedience
by the things which he suffered."*

(Hebrews 5:8)

I'm an amateur gardener and try to raise a wide assortment of fruits, vegetables, and flowers each year. Among my favorites are peaches. Every year my mouth waters as I anticipate the September harvest that yields the delectable, juicy fruit. My father taught me his secret to cultivating large, beautiful peaches.

"I cut out enough of the tree," he said "so when your mother comes out and looks at it, she says, 'Ahh. You killed it.' After the blossoms turn into fruit, it's her turn. She pinches off half to two-thirds of the tiny fruit, to the point that when I see it, I say, 'Ahh. Did you leave any fruit on the tree?'"

The method works for two reasons. First, all peaches develop on new wood, not the previous year's growth. Second, if the fruit grows too close together, they fight for the same space and crowd out the room that would allow them to grow larger. The best fruit comes from trees that are pruned and thinned every single year, even though it appears you're hurting the tree or its crop.

Two years in a row, I neglected my peach tree. The limbs grew tall and gangly. It didn't seem to be a problem because I still had an abundant crop crowded together on tall branches. I figured I'd use a ladder at harvest time and prune the tree the following season. I anticipated the juicy sweetness of ripe peaches and couldn't wait for them to be ready. Three weeks before they finished ripening, two main branches broke under the weight of overloaded fruit on unsupported limbs. We harvested the peaches but lost two-thirds of the tree. Saving the tree required drastic pruning that threatened the next year's crop.

Like the peach tree, Martin's health had proceeded unchecked. Like the peach tree, it required a drastic change. After learning what was wrong and being strengthened by a glimmer of light, the painful process of change began.

Dr. Kinder suggested a procedure on Martin's prostate that might allow his kidneys to rebound. Late in March, Martin and I entered the same-day surgical section of a local hospital. Two-and-a-half weeks had passed since our visit with his primary care physician.

I kissed him goodbye and settled down on a comfortable chair in the waiting room—a room appropriately named. I waited for my loved one to come out of surgery. Waited for each second to tick by and pass the hours ahead of me. Waited and worried.

Would Martin be okay? How effective would the surgery be? What about his recovery? Would he be in a lot of pain? Would surgery fix his problems?

Other fears dragged my mind down a dark spiral. How would we pay for the staggering hospital bill? The front receptionist wanted payment up front, several thousand dollars, for outpatient surgery. I delayed and asked her to have it billed. We didn't have that kind of money. What would we do?

Searching for relief, I opened The Book of Mormon at my bookmark and started reading at Jacob chapter 3. Tension eased, but my heart remained agitated. The very long allegory of the olive tree in chapter 5 beckoned me to continue.

The story became personal. I was the olive tree being pruned and nurtured as I sat in the hospital. Jesus Christ, the Lord of the vineyard, was tackling some of my untamed fruit—impatience, the need to control, putting my never-ending to-do list above all things, and so on. He was cutting out the bad growth and burning it through my current trials. I didn't like it.

In the story, the Lord of the vineyard knew how to produce good fruit. Unlike my failed attempts with the peach tree, when the Lord saw his olive tree decaying, he didn't ignore it. Instead, he said "I will prune it, and dig about it, and nourish it, that perhaps it may shoot forth young and tender branches, and it perish not" (Jacob 5:4). He did this more than once to save his valuable fruit.

Our lives are like both trees. The Lord of our personal vineyards prunes us, digs about us, and nourishes us. The hurtful cultivating process is not the arbitrary act of a vengeful God who wields his tree loppers with wild abandonment.

Instead, the opposite is true. God knows what kind of fruit He wants us to bear, and He knows the exact pruning and digging that will make it so. As Elder Richard G. Scott said, "He therefore gives you experiences that stimulate growth, understanding, and compassion which polish you for your everlasting benefit. To get you from where you are to where He wants you to be requires a lot of stretching, and that generally entails discomfort and pain" ("Trust in the Lord," 16).

I pondered these truths while I waited for Martin, hoping the surgery would succeed, hoping it would mean the end of my current pruning season.

Two hours later, Dr. Kinder approached and ushered me to a quiet corner of the waiting room. "Martin did just fine through the surgery." He drew me a diagram. "He had an enlarged prostate that was part of the problem. I carved it out to relieve pressure from the ureters."

"Does that mean he'll get better? That his kidneys will improve?"

"It's hard to say. Now the bladder is empty, urine won't reflux into the kidneys. They might rebound. His function has already improved since last week. I'm hopeful."

The heavy burden pressing on my shoulder lessened.

"You still need to follow up with a kidney doctor."

I nodded. "We meet with them on the fifth of April."

"Good. Martin will be in recovery for twenty minutes more or so. They'll come and get you when he's awake," he said, and he left.

I closed my eyes, drew in a deep breath, and tasted the sweet fruit of hope. We had discovered the problem that plagued us for years and followed the counsel to take care of it. Now Martin could recover physically. We could recover financially. I could recover emotionally. I was right. The tough pruning, thinning, and shaping appeared to be over.

However, the wise Lord of the vineyard knew we weren't done.

Martin recovered from the operation at home the last days of March. Some of his strength returned, and we expected a full recovery. In the first week of April, we walked through the front office of Nephrology Associates of Utah with eager hearts. Sun reflected off the large windows of the brown building. Buds blossomed on the trees. The warm weather matched my outlook.

Dated blue-green Berber carpet filled a waiting room, complete with fake green plants and uncomfortable chairs. I glanced at the other kidney patients, and noticed most of them were senior citizens. A few appeared to have moderate health. The majority had an unhealthy pallor and looked like they couldn't hold themselves upright without the chair backs.

We didn't belong here. Martin was only fifty-one years old, and he was a strong man with a loud, contagious laugh who loved life. How could we belong in this place where people looked like they barely clung onto their mortal existence?

A glance at Martin's gray countenance and wilted body surfaced doubt. I pushed it down. He hadn't recovered from the surgery. Right? The doubt persisted and wrapped a heavy cloak around me that blocked the sun.

In the examination room, the doctor reviewed Martin's current state. Kidney function had improved a little since the surgery. A little? That was it? What happened to rebounding? To getting better?

"We'll monitor your numbers for two to three months. They might continue to improve. If not, you'll have to consider treatment for kidney failure."

"What are the chances his kidneys will rebound?"

"It's hard to say. We hope for the best, but time will tell."

The cautious, uncommitted answer stripped away the last false hope I had for a season of growth and abundance. The doctors established their baseline of Martin's health from the blood count right after prostate surgery. Never mind the fact that a month had passed since the first lab from Dr. Stevens. That month counted for nothing.

Survival mode kicked in. I wanted to do something, but I didn't know what. Sit back, watch, and wait? That plan of attack was no attack at all. Good things happen to those who make them happen. The doctor's answer didn't fit or go along with that idea.

I understood their caution, but I didn't believe it. They didn't know Martin like I did. My husband had been sick for months before the surgery. This was a chronic problem that needed solved, and I believed transplant was the cure for kidney failure. Why wouldn't they go ahead and just get it taken care of? My cousin had received a transplant after a quick turnaround. Why couldn't Martin?

We left with a referral to meet with one of the clinic's physician assistants. She would talk to us about future treatment options. The sooner we met with her, the more time we'd have to determine the best course for Martin. *If* he needed future treatment, the doctor had emphasized.

If he needed it? I knew the answer. He needed treatment now. Different options? I knew that answer, too. Transplant. Not interested in dialysis. My cousin recounted horror stories about his one-time emergency bout with hemodialysis the week before his transplant. Every instinct told me to avoid that route.

With nothing else we could do, we met with the PA. The meeting gave us good information about dialysis but felt irrelevant to me. I filed it away at the back of my brain, determined we wouldn't need it. A transplant would happen three or four months down the road. The labs from the doctor's office showed he'd improved. He'd be fine until then.

The perfect, warm spring weather changed. Rain fell in the valleys, and snow blanketed the Wasatch Mountains. The cold weather matched a voice message Martin received from the PA two days later. She had the results of the blood draw done the same day as our appointment. The numbers were "significantly worse." He had to start dialysis. Immediately.

Her words infiltrated my bones with more cold than the snow and rain.

April 15, 2011. Another waiting room. Another surgical procedure. This time a nameless doctor inserted a hemodialysis port—the emergency kind, the risky kind. The PICC line entered Martin's body five inches below his collarbone and accessed a vein with a direct route to his heart. If germs, dirt, or other contaminants made their way through the tubing, they could create an infection that might cause death. The doctor emphasized cleanliness and caution.

After the procedure, we crossed the lobby to a dialysis center. Fifteen large recliners lined the edges of an open room, and most of them had people stretched out with their legs elevated, reading or sleeping. Dialyzers, blood purifying machines that were four feet high, stood next to each chair. A low hum filled the still air.

The attending nurse directed Martin to an empty station, and he sat in the recliner. She sanitized the two tubes dangling out of his chest and hooked them to the device next to his chair. Blood flowed out of one tube, into the machine, and back into Martin's body through the other tube.

Martin pulled a lever on the side of the chair to push his legs and feet up. Lines of exhaustion eased as he closed his eyes. I watched my husband with concern. Even a small surgical procedure is draining, and he needed rest. Not to mention the fatigue that wracked his body from limited, almost nonexistent, kidney function.

I grabbed a stool and sat at the bottom of his feet. The machine whirred, and his blood flowed.

A shrill beep pierced the silence. The nurse came over and examined the flashing lights on the machine. Blood had stopped flowing. She wiggled the catheters until movement started.

Martin relaxed again and shifted positions. Ten minutes later, another beep shattered the air.

The nurse returned and adjusted the port. "Try keeping your feet on the floor," she said.

Obedient, Martin lowered the footrest. He reclined back as far as he could with his feet on the floor and tried to relax.

The whirring started again and lasted fifteen minutes. Another beep. Another adjustment. Again and again. In the end, the dialyzer only worked when Martin sat upright, stiff as a board, feet on the floor. Even then, it still stopped and started from time to time.

Three hours later, a session length shorter than future sessions would be, and with an actual filtration time of much less, Martin finished. Lines etched into his face deeper than those he had right after surgery. Weariness tugged his limbs downward and weighted his feet, which shuffled across the linoleum floor as we headed to the door.

"It should get better." The nurse tried to encourage him. "People don't feel well on treatment days but do better on their off days." Her optimistic tone contrasted with the deep despair that accompanied the part of the message I heard: "Don't feel well."

The following Monday, Martin sat in the torture chamber again, this time in Bountiful instead of Salt Lake, where the complications he experienced during his first session with the beastly machine continued as his blood flowed and halted several times. He went back to the clinic on Wednesday and Friday and returned Monday, Wednesday, and Friday the week after that, and the week after that, three days a week, like clockwork.

The routine and problems repeated themselves at each session. A layer of fibrin had formed inside his body near the port opening. It flapped back and forth, blocking the blood flow off and on. Each four-hour period gave him less than three hours of actual dialysis.

Perhaps a new catheter would help. The doctor ordered a replacement—another surgical procedure for Martin.

It didn't help.

The doctors continued to monitor Martin's health. Each week the nurses drew a vial of blood for the labs to check the kidney function. Up. Down. Up. Down. Down. Up.

My emotions bounced around with the lab results. As we waited for the time to pass until the doctors would allow a transplant, I prayed for patience and understanding. And I learned things. And I grew.

In the middle of May, I wrote in my journal, "Things I am Grateful for Because of Martin's Health:"

- I'm learning to be more tolerant, loving, and empathetic to Martin. I'm learning patience and forgiveness. I'm learning to bite my tongue and realize good will return faster if I don't gripe. Martin and I are closer.

- I'm learning to take better care of myself physically, so I'll have the physical, emotional, and mental strength to care for Martin and my children.

- I'm learning how to accept service and not just give it. I know the Savior better because of my debt to all those helping me do things I can't do for myself.

Years later, I didn't remember what I'd written. I considered dialysis a complete waste of three months—an impediment to transplant. They weren't. Because I recorded my experiences, I could recognize the Lord's hand during those dark months. Like President Dieter F. Uchtdorf said, "Often the deep valleys of our present will be understood only by looking back on them from the mountains of our future experience" ("Continue in Patience," 58). When we look back, we can see what we learned and how we grew.

Learning from our trials is a surprising mirror to Jesus Christ. The Apostle Paul wrote, "Though he were a Son, yet learned he obedience by the things which he suffered" (Hebrews 5:8). Ease and comfort without distress and difficulties didn't have full sway over the Savior's entire life before the atonement. Rather, His life was full of trials that taught Him.

Before Gethsemane and Calvary, Satan tempted Him in the wilderness. Jewish leaders rejected Him and tried to kill Him on multiple occasions. The residents of His home town of Nazareth scorned Him. Through it all, He suffered, He learned, He grew. He gained what He needed in order to accomplish the atonement and the resurrection. In the end, He became a perfect, exalted being, like our Heavenly Father.

Like Jesus, we learn to be more like our Heavenly Father through the pain of being cut back and cultivated. As President Russell M. Nelson said, "The process of perfection includes challenges to overcome and steps to repentance that may be very painful" ("Perfection Pending," 86).

We can endure great adversities if we believe the end reward will be worth it. As Latter-day Saints, we know our reward will be worth it—even though we can't see it right now. The Lord said, "Ye cannot behold with your natural eyes, . . . the design of your God concerning those things which shall come hereafter, and the glory which shall follow after much tribulation" (Doctrine and Covenants 58:3). We know that if we remain faithful, the end is the sweetest, most abundant fruit of all—exaltation.

However, just knowing there is purpose to our trials doesn't mean they're easy. They aren't, but we have help. Like the gardener who returned again and again to his olive vineyard, the Lord is always there to help. Jesus Christ strengthened my back and shared my burden over the coming weeks and months while we dealt with the devastating impact of Martin's illness.

CHAPTER 5

FEELING FORSAKEN

"Why hast Thou forsaken me?"

(Matthew 27:46)

The bell dinged and filled me with the excitement only a five-year-old can get out of riding an elevator. Metal doors slid open. I filed into the small space after my family. My older sister, Sharon, held my younger brother Neil's right hand, and I grasped his left hand. She drew us behind her into the elevator while Mom pushed the button to take us to the tenth floor. The very top floor of the Tribune Building in Salt Lake City.

It was time for our annual visit to the dentist. It was such an exciting time because we got to travel to Salt Lake City. Once we arrived in the waiting area, I could stare out of the window at the ant-sized people from a million feet above. And the very best part of the adventure was the exciting voyage of riding an elevator high enough to reach heaven.

The box jerked us upward. I smiled even though my stomach stayed put while the rest of my body went up, up, up.

A moment later it stopped with a lurch and the doors slid open. Mom and Dad walked out. Sharon led Neil out, pulling us along in a straight line. Still holding hands with my brother, I followed him, the caboose in our little train. Before I could cross the track separating the small compartment from the lobby, enormous steel doors rushed toward our clutched hands. I dropped Neil's hand to avoid getting crushed by the beast. Like snapping teeth, the doors closed two seconds later, encasing me inside. Alone.

Terror seized my mind. The awful monster jolted, moved, and descended with me trapped inside. Deserted. Abandoned. At the mercy of who knew what. Sobs wracked my body. The long ride ended, and steel jaws opened to spit me out of its cavernous mouth and into the unknown without my family, with no one to help.

An elderly gentleman in a suit stood in the lobby. He surveyed the scene and smiled. The kind angel ushered me to stand near a wall and waited with me. We held hands. The strength of his large palm enfolded my tiny fingers in warmth.

Mere seconds later, fast pounding steps echoed through the stairwell and filled the cavernous lobby. An urgent, frantic voice grabbed my attention. "Michelle!" The sound bounced off the marble walls, and I turned toward it. Dad raced through the lobby toward me.

"Daddy!" I threw myself into his embrace.

"It's all right. I'm here. I've got you."

My terror fled. He'd come. He'd rescued me from the fate decreed by the awful monster. My cries quieted. Dad thanked my guardian angel and took me into the elevator once again. He made sure I was safe and secure the entire ride back to the tenth floor.

Being alone and abandoned is a feeling most of us can relate to. Though not physically deserted like I was in the elevator, I often felt forsaken and frightened as our family moved into a world with Martin on dialysis. My mind whirled with emotions I couldn't process. Better not to think. Instead, I focused on doctor appointments, kids' homework, meals that fit Martin's new dietary restrictions, and the puzzle of medical billing and insurance. I just kept busy. It worked.

Kind of.

Until normal bumps interrupted my fragile routine.

A week after Martin started dialysis, the basement shower head broke. Water poured down the walls and onto the floors.

My heart tightened in my stomach. What could I do? It had to be repaired before our nineteen-year-old daughter, Katie, returned home from college the following week. The shower shared a wall with her closet, and she couldn't use the closet in that condition. Who was going to fix it? Martin always handled the home repairs, but he was too sick and couldn't do it. We had no money to pay a plumber. There was no way I could do it. Despair filled my thoughts.

Our older sons, William and Adam, came to the rescue. Neither of them lived at home, but they planned to come for the weekend and fix the shower under Martin's direction. They worked on it while I traveled to Ephraim, Utah, to bring Katie back home to Bountiful, Utah.

When I pulled into the parking lot outside her apartment, Katie sprang up the steps, her strawberry blonde hair bouncing side to side as she ran to hug me. My arms tightened around her slender frame and held her tight for a brief moment.

We hauled box after box up the half-flight of stairs from her basement apartment to the minivan. The volume of boxes, clothes, and small pieces of furniture I needed to transport home was staggering. I needed Martin, because 3D-Tetris was his specialty, not mine. He could pack everything any college girl owned into a smaller space than anyone deemed possible. Why did I have to do this alone?

Straightening my shoulders, I channeled my husband and thought about how he might arrange the boxes. Together, Katie and I maneuvered each one into the back of the van. The trunk door squeezed the last of them when it shut, but we got everything in the car. Mission accomplished. With a wave at Katie's roommates, we climbed into the only space left and headed home.

During the drive, Katie related story after story about her roommates, their antics, and the fun they had together. Energy bounced around the van and eased my weary mind. As I listened to her animated voice, I pushed slow, deep breaths out of my chest and allowed them to carry away some of my tension. It would be so nice to have her home for the summer. Her bright personality would fill the house with sunshine. Everything was going to be all right. We'd get through this.

The miles flew by, and before we knew it, we pulled into the driveway. Home. Slightly rejuvenated, I made my way to Katie's bedroom. She dashed into the house after me in search of her dad.

"Daddy? Daddy, I'm home." Arms full, she bounced down the stairs, abandoned her load in the family room and hurried toward the conversation and laughter that drifted from the bedroom. At the doorway, she halted, frozen in place.

Martin lay on her bed wearing a bathrobe, his face gray. Voices pulled her attention to the closet where her two older brothers worked on the broken shower. Alone. Without her dad standing beside them to show them how to cut pipes, guide their eager hands, and teach them the proper way to repair plumbing. Katie faltered. Her eyes moved from her brothers to Martin. Her mouth dropped, and her body went rigid.

"How are you, Katie Kate?" Martin said with a weak smile. He shifted and opened his arms. "I've missed you."

All bounce gone, Katie crossed the room, bent down, and gave him a tentative hug. "I've missed you, too," she said, her voice quiet.

"Dad?" William drew Martin's attention away from his daughter and back to the closet. "Now what?"

William held a pipe wrench in a thick, firm hand. Short, dirty blond hair dripped with water that had sprayed when he and Adam had cut into the pipe.

"Should I go get the plumber's tape now?" Adam asked. His dark hair, a couple inches longer than his brother's, was also wet. Water fell off his bangs and landed on his nose. A mischievous grin stole across Adam's face. Out of the corner of his eye, he looked at his brother, just two years older than him. With one swift movement, he flung his head toward William. Droplets flew off his soaked hair and landed on his brother.

"Hey." William laughed and pushed his brother.

I rolled my eyes. Some things never changed. It didn't matter that they were both in their mid-twenties and that Adam had married a year earlier. They teased each other now, just as they had while growing up.

With a laugh, I turned to Katie. "Come on. Let's get the rest of your stuff."

A quiet, dumbfounded girl retreated and escaped upstairs to grab another box.

"Mom . . ." she said, tugging at a box in the back of the van. Wedged into the back, it wouldn't budge without the kind of effort she didn't have. My daughter crumpled next to it. "Dad's not . . ."

"Oh, honey." I put my arms around her. "We tried to tell you. He's sick."

"Yes. I know you said he's sick, but . . . he didn't act this way four weeks ago when I was home."

"He had dialysis today. Treatment days are bad. He won't be as sick tomorrow."

"But . . . I didn't realize . . ." She stopped.

My heart ached. What could I say? How could I make it better? I didn't have answers. Anything I'd say might appear a platitude, so I didn't say anything, and we unloaded the van in silence before joining the others while they worked.

Later in the afternoon, Brian arrived home from his job as a life-guard and poked his blond head into the room to see what was going on. After changing out of his uniform, he joined his brothers. His smile and attempts to join the party seemed hollow.

Brian had said little about the situation with Martin. What was he thinking? What emotions was he bottling up? He'd already lost one parent. He was only two when his birth mother had passed. Though he had no memories of Sherri, Brian felt a keen void in his life.

Her death left scars on an all her children, William, Adam, Katie, and Brian. With Martin sick, I couldn't imagine the pain of their thoughts and emotions. They had to be watching and wondering as another parent's health worsened each day. Did they fear losing another parent?

The afternoon passed. I watched Martin's strength ebb, even though he spent most of the time resting on the bed. I watched my sons cut, solder, and mend with unskilled eagerness to help. I watched Katie retreat further with each minute. I watched Brian try to join in, to bridge the gap between torment and peace.

It didn't seem fair to ask this of my family. Where was God? Had he forsaken Martin? My children? Me?

Emotions such as these are common. Health fails. Loved ones die or leave the church. Disabilities affect emotional or physical life. Cherished dreams crumble and fall around our feet. Everyone's trial of being forsaken is unique, but the struggle can cause us to wonder where the Lord is and why He disappeared from view. The Prophet Joseph cried unto God in distress, "O God, where art thou? And where is the pavilion that covereth thy hiding place?" (D&C 121:1).

Feeling forsaken also mirrors the Savior. Jesus Christ—the God of the universe—experienced the agony of losing the sustaining help of the Spirit in His final hours. As He hung on the cross, He cried in agony, "My God, my God, why hast thou forsaken me?" (Matthew 27:46; Mark 15:34).

Although we may feel alone, it's important to realize we are not, and neither was the Savior. Elder Jeffrey R. Holland declared, "With all the conviction of my soul I testify that . . . a perfect Father did not forsake His Son in that hour. Indeed, it is my personal belief that in all of Christ's mortal ministry the Father may never have been closer to His Son than in these agonizing final moments of suffering. Nevertheless, . . . the Father briefly withdrew from Jesus the comfort of His Spirit" ("None Were with Him," 87). Just as Heavenly Father stayed with His Only Begotten Son, He will stay with us, His children.

If the Lord is with us, why do we often feel alone? Sometimes the Lord withdraws His spirit to allow us the freedom to choose what we will do. This, too, is a mirror of our Savior. As Elder Robert D. Hales explained, "so that [Jesus] could finally demonstrate that He was choosing for Himself, He was left alone. . . . He exercised His agency to act, enduring to the end, until He could say, 'It is finished'" ("Agency," 25).

During our sorrow and trials, our family made the choice to press forward, to pray for the ability to endure, and to have faith in the eternal plan of salvation. Both Martin and I reached out to our children and encouraged them, hugged them, let them cry, and reminded them God loves them and is in charge. I prayed with and for Martin, loved him, and served him. Our family accepted service from others. I moved forward in faith, believing Christ would be there for me, just as my dad was for me all those years earlier.

We trusted Jesus would succor us in our infirmities (see Alma 7:12). The word succor comes from a Latin root that means to "run to help, hasten to the aid of" (Online Etymology Dictionary). Just as my father sprinted down ten flights of stairs to come to my aid, the Savior ran to help me, to succor me.

Though I didn't see it then, later I realized the Lord was running to our aid the whole time. He sent our sons to fix the broken shower and other mishaps, like the starter motor in my car. He sent neighbors with random meals and treats left on the doorstep. He gave me a weekend retreat with my mother and sisters, where I could both laugh and cry with those who loved me.

The Lord helped Martin too. As the nurse said on the first day, Martin's ability to handle his treatments increased. Dialysis always sapped his strength, but on his days off, he grew stronger. After a few weeks, he could work again, and we spent several hours together painting vacated rental units. Martin organized a leadership conference for youth leaders. He spent time and energy talking with and nurturing me and our children.

We stayed the course. As we did, we drew upon the Savior's grace and mercy, which gave us a greater ability to choose Him. It wasn't always easy. The journey of staying the course when you feel alone can take months of praying, struggling, and searching. The journey was hard for our children, and they all found strength in their own ways and time.

A year after the episode with the basement shower, Katie sat in her stake president's office for the final interview to submit her mission papers. She told us later that as he looked across his desk at her, his words conveyed the impression that she was a naïve girl, unfamiliar with tumultuous storms that can drag a person down.

"Katie, you have led an innocent life free from serious transgression," he said. "Many of the people you will teach will have experiences full of sin and sorrow. How will you testify to them of the atonement of Jesus Christ?"

With boldness, she related she knew God because of the trials she'd been through, trials of losing her birth mother, trials of witnessing her father's illness, trials of praying for strength to get through transplant. God didn't remove all her struggles, and she still lived with their impact. But He strengthened her. He helped her begin to "bear up [her] burdens with ease," and to submit "with patience to all the will of the Lord" (Mosiah 24:15). She testified God comes to you in your hardships, and He strengthens you as you endure them.

The Savior loves us and wants to help us. He is always there. We can always reach out to Him and feel His love.

The elevator story is as a treasured memory. I know it terrified me then, but I only remember that on a logical level. When I reminisce about that experience, I feel anew the love of being found. So it will be with our lives. When we reflect on our trials, we can gain a perspective that might have eluded us during the actual event. We can open our hearts to the Savior's embrace and remember how He runs through the lobby to save us. We can rejoice in the love of being found by Him.

Yet knowing God will gather us in mercy and never forsake us doesn't always make it easy while we are struggling. One of the hardest things for me was the toll that Martin's health took on him and my children. As a wife and mother, I suffered their pain and agonized alongside them in the weeks that followed.

CHAPTER 6

CHRIST CARRIES OUR BURDENS

"Surely he hath borne our griefs,
and carried our sorrows . . ."

(Isaiah 53:4)

If you've ever lived where it snows, chances are you've driven in the middle of a storm that was nerve-wracking, frightening, dangerous, or all of the above. Icy, slick roads provide plenty of fodder for war stories we tell to our children when warning them about snow-driving or when we share with friends during an I'll-one-up-you session.

I remember once such time when thick, heavy snow blanketed the outside world in silence and carpeted the roads in a slick veneer. I was driving home from a church meeting on a street that had a slight incline, barely noticeable most of the time. On that day, however, the incline morphed into a steep, upward angle of ninety degrees or more and dared my old sedan to finish the climb.

Half a block from home, the wheels lost traction and spun. The car slowed and then refused to move forward anymore despite my pleadings to it and prayers to God, both silent and spoken. My heart pounded and kept rhythm with the fast-paced wiper blades that were losing the battle as the snow piled on my windshield. I gripped the steering wheel tighter, held my breath, and hoped I wouldn't careen off the road. Believing that a lower gear would help, I downshifted to second and found a little more purchase, but not enough. The car slid backwards.

At that moment, a neighbor and his son, who were shoveling the six inches of snow off their driveway, came to my rescue. With heads down and gloved hands on my trunk, they shouldered the burden of my car. Their brute force added to the small momentum I could get from the gas, and they pushed me up the hill. Without the help of my neighbors, I would have had to abandon my car on the side of the road where it would have interfered with the snowplows that ran up and down the streets during the rest of the day as the skies dumped snow on our world. All of my efforts were not enough. I needed help.

All of us have times when the burdens of life are too difficult to handle, when we're stretched to the maximum of our ability, when we cannot move on without help. The storm we traveled through when Martin started dialysis threatened to careen me off the road several times.

Oddly enough, Sunday, the day of peace and rest, was harder than the rest of the week. Relief Society, Sunday School, and sacrament meeting all spoke of faith, hope, mercy, and grace—all things I didn't feel.

Martin was home in bed, and I sat with the kids alone, worrying, buried under the weight of the blizzard in our lives that obliterated the beautiful May weather and dimmed the brilliant sun outside. During sacrament meeting, Katie leaned against the wall that bordered the aisle bench where we sat. Her eyes were shut and her face sagged—a new normal for her since she moved home.

Nicole sat next to me and leaned her head on my shoulder. Brown curls fell into her eyes, and she swiped at them with a quick jerk. I stroked her hair. Three months earlier, she'd turned twelve, and on her birthday, Martin and I took her to the temple to perform baptisms for the dead in the Salt Lake Temple. That had been a happy day. We hadn't realized the storm brewing on the horizon, although the dark clouds were visible even then.

Our youngest son, Dennis, squirmed on the bench as he sat on the other side of me. Sacrament meeting was the last meeting in our three-hour block. After two hours of Church, his active eight-year-old body refused to hold still.

"Shh. It's time for the sacrament," I said.

Movement shifted from his body to his hands, and he fiddled with a random toy he'd stashed in his pocket before he walked out the door for church. I placed my hand on top of his to stop the action. Resigned, he flopped across my lap, and I rubbed his back while the music played.

The chorister raised her arm and signaled the congregation to begin the reverent sacrament hymn. For two measures, I sang in praise and hope to my Savior before my voice cracked and forced me to stop. Eyes shut, I fought back tears. The congregation carried the words through the chapel to my aching soul. Words of faith and hope attacked my heart rather than provide comfort.

I knew the Savior succored me. Then why was it so hard? Was it me? If I trusted Him more, would my burdens be less heavy? Would I feel more peace during this struggle? If I had more faith, would the storm end or at least be less treacherous?

The song ended, and I looked toward the sacrament table. Our son Brian unfolded his tall frame from the bench and knelt behind the white tablecloth. He bent his head and picked up the microphone. With a soft voice, he spoke the words of the sacred prayer, a voice that had become too quiet at home.

The prayer ended, and I kept my head bowed and hid my face behind my long hair to keep the ward members from seeing me cry. A young hand pushed a tray in front of me. Broken bread. The Savior had a broken body. He was there for me. I had to find Him.

A few minutes later, the water tray arrived. The Savior bled and died for me. He, too, had wept in agony. He shrank from the bitter cup. It wasn't easy for Him. Was it okay that it wasn't easy for me?

Of course, it was okay. Though my mind knew the logical answer, my aching heart struggled to accept it. As the sacred ordinance progressed, a stillness, soft and quiet as winter snow that dampened the noises of the world, wrapped my spirit in peace, strength, and security that spring day. My Savior knew me, and each week during the sacrament, He eased my burdens enough for me to continue moving forward without slipping off the road.

All too soon, though, the blinding, raging storms of worries, agonies, and burdens would reassert themselves throughout the week and blot out the sun. One of the heavy burdens both Martin and I wrestled with was helping our children understand what was happening. Neither of us wanted his treatments to frighten them, so we talked about them as if they were a natural, common occurrence. We invited each of them to visit Martin at the dialysis center to see what he did at the clinic and remove some of the mystery.

One day, I asked our youngest two, Nicole and Dennis, if they wanted to go visit Martin at the center. Nicole shook her head.

"Come on. It's not scary. We won't be long."

During the five-minute drive, I tried to prep the children, so they'd know what to expect. At the clinic, Dennis moved ahead of Nicole toward the chair where Martin sat, hesitant, but his scientific mind was still fascinated. Nicole hung back, clung to my hand, and pressed her body close to mine.

"Look, see? It's not scary at all," I said. They didn't believe me.

Martin showed them the gigantic machine, taller than Dennis and almost as tall as Nicole, but not quite. Soft whirring escaped from its front panel, deceitful in its sounds of comfort. Tubing filled with bright red blood stretched from Martin's catheter ports and hooked into the machine. Dennis's enthusiasm dropped at the sight of flowing blood, and his fidgeting ceased.

"Does it do all your blood?" he asked.

"Yes. Several times," Martin said. As he explained how it worked, both kids looked shy and uncomfortable.

"Can we go now?" Nicole said, her body still pressed tight against mine.

"Yes. Give your dad a hug."

Wide eyes looked up at me. "Is it okay? What about the tubes?"

"It's fine, Nicole," Martin said. "See, I can move a little without bothering them." He opened his arms to receive a hug.

After a quick embrace, she tugged on my arm to leave. Neither child ever went back. They were so innocent, so pure. How would they be at the end of all this? Would the scars of these experiences drag them down for the rest of their lives?

It didn't seem fair that innocent people had to live with wounds they didn't deserve. Truthfully, it isn't fair; it isn't just; it isn't right. But it is a fact of life that mirrors the Savior's life. Elder Jeffrey R. Holland said, "The wounds in His hands, feet, and side are signs that in mortality painful things happen even to the pure and the perfect, signs that tribulation is not evidence that God does not love us. It is a significant and hopeful fact that it is the wounded Christ who comes to our rescue" (*Christ and the New Covenant*, 259).

As much as I wanted "having more faith" to be the solution that would end the storm, remove my heartache, and leave me peaceful and happy, life doesn't work that way. It wasn't designed that way. Christ had perfect faith, and He still had to endure hardships. The faith that took Him through the atonement did not replace the agony of Gethsemane and the cross with happiness while He was going through them.

Rather, having faith means we trust the wounded Christ to succor us and help us overcome, endure, or wait patiently for some future date when the blizzard ends and peace returns. It took many years for me to realize that having faith did not equal zero pain. Yet, even though I didn't fully comprehend that truth then, just knowing that the Savior, too, had been wounded helped me press forward each day.

The days faded from one into another, and a steady routine brought an illusion of normalcy. At last, the first week of June arrived. Martin had been on dialysis for six weeks, which meant we were six weeks closer for the doctors to okay a transplant.

The last day of school brought relief to all of us, me included. Brian finished his junior year, and Dennis completed second grade. Both ended the year with a shrug that expressed gratitude for a summer break. Nicole's last day of school, however, was big. She was leaving elementary school.

Sixth grade graduation. Friday, June 3. Dialysis Day.

In the morning, Martin hugged his daughter and apologized for not being able to attend the ceremony. We waved at him as he drove to the clinic.

Nicole put on her best Sunday dress for the program. She asked me to straighten her hair and get rid of her unfashionable curls. She wanted to look special on this big day.

I arrived early and walked into the tan, glazed-brick cafeteria. Several parents already sat on brown folding chairs crammed close together. After locating an open seat, I waited for the program to begin. And missed Martin.

All year long, Martin had enjoyed going to his children's programs and events. He attended all parent-teacher conferences. He was one of the few fathers who could attend the sixth grade Halloween and Valentine's Day dances to help even out the boy-to-girl ratio. Nicole loved that because then she didn't have to dance with the boys. Of all the events he had to miss, it was graduation.

Bit by bit the room filled. At the appointed hour, the students filed in and took their pre-assigned places in the front rows. The kids sang sentimental songs of hope. The three classroom teachers presented awards for students who earned top grades, met presidential fitness goals, and had perfect attendance. None were for Nicole.

Toward the end of the program, Nicole's teacher took the microphone.

"The last award is a special district award. It goes to the individual who made the most progress in reading this year. Only one person in the entire district will receive it."

I didn't pay this announcement much heed. Nicole battled a mild learning disability and had spent her grade school years behind her peers.

"Nicole Christensen, please come forward."

My jaw dropped, and my eyes raced to look at her. If anyone deserved this prestigious award, she did. I knew hard how she'd fought to learn to read because I'd been with her every painful step of the way. She struggled to read, and I struggled with her. For two years I tutored her at school during the class's reading hour. We switched to a professional tutor in Salt Lake City, and three days a week I drove Nicole twenty-five minutes one-way before school to meet with them. She practiced reading to me hour after hour. She agonized over each syllable, and I agonized with her as I pointed to the words, coached her to sound out the vowels, and encouraged her to keep trying. Through it all, Nicole's love of books and stories was strong.

Nicole looked as shocked as I felt. She moved to the front, took her award, and returned to her seat, with an enormous smile plastered across her face.

Once the ceremony ended, we took a million pictures. In each one, she held her certificate and grinned. Behind the camera, I beamed as well.

As soon as Martin got home, she threw her arms around him with a tight hug.

"Guess what, Dad? I got an award. And you'll never guess what. It's for reading."

"That's so exciting. Congratulations."

"I wish you'd been there," she said.

"I know. Me too. But I'm here now. Let's go party."

Even though Martin hadn't been there to watch her receive the honor, he celebrated. He, too, had shared her burden and helped her read. He comprehended the significance of this victory and rejoiced with his daughter.

Nicole wanted to go to In-N-Out Burgers—and eat inside. With only her dad and me sitting at the table, she had all the attention on herself. She recited the details of the day, happy and excited. The evening ended full of love.

My experiences of bearing the burden with Nicole mirror the way the Savior suffers with us. He took upon Him our infirmities (see Alma 7:11–12). What we suffer, He suffers. What we agonize over, He agonizes over. "Surely, he hath borne our griefs, and carried our sorrows" (Isaiah 53:4). Every. Single. One.

Elder David A. Bednar said, "There is no physical pain, no spiritual wound, no anguish of soul or heartache, no infirmity or weakness you or I ever confront in mortality that the Savior did not experience first" ("Bear Up Their Burdens with Ease," 90).

There is an important distinction between my suffering with Nicole and the Savior's with us. Although I hurt with her, I didn't completely understand what she went through. The Savior, on the other hand, *does* comprehend. As Elder Bednar further explained, "the Son of God perfectly knows and understands, for He has felt and borne our individual burdens. And because of His infinite and eternal sacrifice (see Alma 34:14), He has perfect empathy and can extend to us His arm of mercy" (90).

The Lord's perfect empathy reaches beyond sharing only our sorrows. He doesn't just keep us from careening off the road or push us out of the snowbanks. He travels the roads with us when the sun is shining, and the birds are singing. He shares our good times, just like we did with Nicole. He applauds our small wins, and He delights in our huge successes.

Because I had struggled with Nicole, I comprehended the depth of her success. Her victory was my victory. So it is with the Savior. Because He struggles alongside us, because He celebrates with us, because He knows everything we go through, our sorrows and joys and achievements are His sorrows and joys and achievements. His greatest triumph will be when we—through Him—receive the ultimate prize of exaltation.

But that ultimate prize is a long way off, and there are bumps and delays. Sometimes we are positive our progress has come to an abrupt halt, just like the delays in Martin's progress toward a transplant.

CHAPTER 7

WAITING ON THE LORD

"He abode two days still in the
same place where he was."

(John 11:6)

When our youngest son, Dennis, was just a few months old, I decided I had not given birth to a boy but to a fish. Even as an infant, he loved the water. True, many babies love to splash in a shallow bathtub, but Dennis out-splashed every child I'd ever seen. As he grew older, I worried because he had no idea that water could be dangerous.

The summer before he turned three, I enrolled both of us in a mom-and-tots swim class. I got in the shallow end with the other moms, stood where the water reached my chest, and held Dennis in front of me with him facing toward me. On cue, I followed the teacher's directions and said, "hold your breath." Then I inhaled, pinched my lips together, and squeezed my eyes shut to show him what to do. Once I demonstrated the act, I released my son, let him sink, and pulled him out of the water.

As expected, he sputtered, coughed, and cried a little. Chubby legs wrapped around my middle and refused to budge. The instructor wanted me to repeat the process so Dennis could learn what to do if he ever fell into a swimming pool without an adult next to him. That didn't happen.

No matter what I did, he wouldn't release his death grip for me to try again. Swimming lessons taught him water was scary. During the course, we never progressed to the lesson about doggy paddling to the side of the pool.

Surprisingly, he still loved the water, but only when his feet touched the bottom. If I took him to the local swimming pool, he'd play for hours on the big water toy. But whenever I tried helping him with a back-float, his legs wrapped around my middle and refused to budge. Even swimming lessons from a skilled instructor failed because he couldn't get past the security he felt with his feet anchored to something solid.

Years passed, and the terror remained strong. The timing wasn't right for my little fish to learn how to swim. If we had rushed him, the process might have cemented the fear deep into his psyche, never to leave. We had to wait.

Waiting. I hate waiting. But just like Dennis needed to wait for swimming lessons, we had to wait for a transplant. Martin and I were ready for it to happen back in April when he first started dialysis. The doctors didn't agree.

If they rushed into a transplant, it might cause an unnecessary surgery, complete with all the risks and pain of an operation. Not to mention it would add the problems of a foreign organ that his body would have to cope with forever. "Transplant is only a treatment not a cure," they told us. It would be far better if his kidneys could rebound.

I didn't see it that way. All I saw were the delays brought about by medical red tape. Martin had been sick for years, and a deep fear nagged at the back of my head. What if they declared Martin better without him being well? I was afraid because I knew the Lord sometimes asks us to do hard things.

I witnessed that with Martin's sister, Jean, whose husband battled liver cancer the same time Martin was on dialysis. Jean and Rolf had fought his illness with intense chemotherapy. In June they faced the ugly truth that it hadn't worked, and Rolf only had days left to live.

"Why is it God requires a greater sacrifice of some than others?" My journal entry after I heard the devastating news about Rolf captured my dread. "I'm so afraid the Lord will require of me a greater sacrifice than I want to give. I'm afraid the sacrifice required is poor health for Martin in the future, just like we've had the past several years."

With my limited knowledge, I was convinced transplant was the cure, the only way we would have a normal life. I was sure of it. However, we had no control. Until the doctors agreed the timing was right, we had to wait.

Despite the emotional toll that waiting took on me, life didn't pause on convenient hold until the storm passed. I couldn't wait for peace and tranquility to arrive before I resumed normal responsibilities. No. My church calling with the Cub Scouts required weekly activities. I had regular articles to write for my part-time Internet marketing job as a content writer. Martin had a myriad of extra doctor appointments I attended with him.

And summer swimming lessons at the local recreational center beckoned. Deep inside, despite the turmoil of our lives, I knew Dennis's waiting period was over. I enrolled him in lessons.

Meanwhile, Martin suffered on dialysis.

On dialysis he stayed alive. Barely. Among other things, his weekly labs showed he was severely anemic, which helped explain his constant fatigue. That seemed a simple problem to fix. Give him more iron.

To my dismay, the doctor explained why it wasn't that simple and why extra doses of iron wouldn't make a difference. Healthy kidneys produce a hormone that stimulates red blood cell production, and damaged kidneys don't produce enough. To compensate, dialysis patients received a synthetic version called Epogen. Because it was so expensive, the established medical protocol and insurance regulations stated that patients were only to receive enough to keep them alive, not enough to make them feel better.

I couldn't believe it. Money. It all boiled down to money and how expensive it was to give someone good health. I prayed for a transplant, even as the waiting continued.

Just as the doctors required us to wait, the Lord often requires us to wait. He had me wait until I was in my thirties to meet Martin. He delayed immediate resolution for Katie as she battled her fears over Martin's health.

In reality, it's not a strange thing for the Lord to ask us to wait. We see an example of this in the Gospel of John when Lazarus was very sick. His sisters, Mary and Martha, sent a message to Jesus and asked Him to come to their aid. They knew He could heal their brother. When Christ received the message, He didn't pack up and leave that instant. Instead, "he abode two days still in the same place where he was" (John 11:6).

I can imagine the distress that Mary and Martha felt wondering why the Lord didn't come. It was urgent. Didn't Jesus know that?

I could relate. Waiting has never been my favorite game. I'm a planner, a person of action. If something isn't happening, I do what I can to make it happen. However, I can't always do something about it. Just as I had to wait on Dennis for swimming and just as I had to wait on the medical world, sometimes I have to wait on the Lord.

President Dieter F. Uchtdorf said, "Every one of us is called to wait in our own way. We wait for answers to prayers. We wait for things which at the time may appear so right and so good to us that we can't possibly imagine why Heavenly Father would delay the answer" ("Continue in Patience," 58).

The Lord asks us to wait for many reasons. Maybe, as with Lazarus, God has a higher purpose to fulfill. Maybe He wants us to learn patience, to learn to trust Him and His timing. Maybe it's as simple as the fact that we aren't ready when we think we are.

I can understand this more when I think about Dennis and his swimming lessons. Dennis hadn't been ready at the ages of three, four, five, six, or seven. Instead, he needed to become comfortable with the water. Rather than forcing futile lessons on him during those years, I took him to the swimming pool to play. Water splashed on his face when he went down the kiddie slide, played on the big toy, or stood in the middle of the waterfall. Bit by bit he ventured deeper and deeper into the water, and over time, his fear departed.

President Uchtdorf continued, "God's promises are not always fulfilled as quickly as or in the way we might hope; they come according to His timing and in His ways" (58). Until the timing is right, though, He will give us as much as He can, just like we did with Dennis's fear of the water.

Looking back at the months right after Martin's initial diagnosis, I can see that Dr. Conrad, Martin's kidney doctor, did the same for Martin. He gave him as much as he could while still keeping within the established protocol that his medical license required.

Early in June, I joined Martin at the clinic for a monthly doctor appointment. Martin's treatment had just ended when I got there, and the CNA ushered us back to an examination room.

Dr. Conrad entered a few minutes later. A trendy dress shirt peeked from underneath his lab coat. He sat and crossed his legs as he looked at Martin's latest labs, revealing patterned socks and shiny brown leather dress shoes. Dr. Conrad was good at what he did, and his dress reflected his success. He stayed on the cutting edge of both fashion and medical research. This was clear each visit as the doctor discussed questions that arose from our own study.

Both Martin and I read as much on the Internet as possible to understand his condition. Martin read several scientific articles that went way above my head, and he talked about each of them with the doctor. Every time, the doctor nodded, smiled, and commented on the article that he, too, had read. Dr. Conrad applied his research to his practice. He was so good that half of his working time he spent with the transplant team at the hospital. We had a lot of confidence in this man and felt blessed that God had helped us find him.

"How are you feeling?" Dr. Conrad said, and he turned his gaze away from the computer screen to focus on Martin.

"Tired. All the time. Especially the days I have treatments," said Martin.

"Hemodialysis is hard on your body. No one feels good the day they come in. Are your off days any better?"

"Some. I'm still exhausted all the time."

"Unfortunately, that's normal," he said. Compassion and kindness laced his voice. "The good news is that your numbers are moving in a good direction."

I processed the words with mixed emotions. On the surface, that sounded good. Better kidney performance meant a better chance of recovery. At least that was the way it was supposed to work. I didn't see that happening. The numbers improved, but Martin did not. His kidney function never got better than about ten percent.

"Have you ever considered peritoneal dialysis?" Dr. Conrad asked. "Most people do better with this form of treatment."

We knew very little about it. He told us that PD, short for peritoneal dialysis, didn't pump blood in and out of a person. Instead, it used fluid in the abdominal cavity to filter the impurities out of the blood. It was easier on the body, and Martin could do it at home. The drawback was that it required yet another surgery to insert a catheter into his abdomen, by which the fluid could be pumped in and out of his body.

Martin was ready to try it, but I met the news with mixed emotions. If he switched to a different form of dialysis—one that was so complicated it required surgery—did that mean they were not considering him for transplant? If he said yes to PD, was he saying no to transplant? Would we have to live with dialysis for the rest of his life until he succumbed to a premature death?

"But what about a transplant?" I asked. "If he does this, would it disqualify him?"

"No." The answer was definite. "PD is a good option. The process to get a transplanted kidney generally takes a minimum of six months from start to finish. That's enough time for the peritoneal dialysis."

Six months? That long? Based on my cousin's experience of receiving a transplant, I expected it would be a month, at most six weeks. I didn't want to wait six more months. I'd waited long enough. Every single day I thought about transplant, and they hadn't even decided whether Martin qualified. I had been counting down the days until three months passed and they would admit his condition was chronic. Now the doctor told me that once the three months were over, that wasn't the end.

"We were hoping to get a transplant in 2011." I said, pushing Dr. Conrad. "Martin's health insurance is only $500 away from the out-of-pocket maximum."

Dr. Conrad paused and then shrugged. "We can initiate the transplant process." He looked back at Martin. "If you improve to the point you feel better, we can put a hold on it. If not, then it's started."

Based on his experience and knowledge, Dr. Conrad could see that waiting longer wasn't necessary. Enough time had passed that had produced enough data. Our period of waiting in a void was ending.

I smiled my thanks to the doctor, prayed my thanks to the Lord later in the day, and emailed the news to our family and friends a couple of days later: "I am so grateful! I truly believe the power of the priesthood and all the fasting and prayers on our behalf are bringing a miracle in Martin's life. Thank you all so much."

The doctor met us where we were when he recommended better dialysis and started the transplant process. His actions mirrored the way the Savior works with us, who always meets us where we are. When Jesus finally arrived at Martha's house, she was distraught at her brother's death. Jesus didn't brush aside her concerns, knowing what He was about to do. Instead, "Jesus wept" with Martha (John 11:35).

Meeting us at our current place is a pattern of His greatness that He has repeated over and over. A good example is how He dealt with the ancient Israelites. God didn't abandon them when they rejected the higher law Moses brought them from Mount Sinai. Instead, He gave them a law they could keep, one designed to prepare them for the greater light of the full gospel.

God does the same thing on our behalf. When we're in a waiting pattern, the Lord meets us where we are. He offers what comfort and help He can regardless of why our progress is stopped. He gives us as much as He can as quickly as He can. Elder Richard G. Scott said, "Your Father in Heaven and His Beloved Son love you perfectly. They would not require you to experience a moment more of difficulty than is absolutely needed for your personal benefit or for that of those you love" ("Trust in the Lord," 17). As soon as all aspects are ready, God will open doors that will help us move forward.

During the summer of dialysis—the summer of waiting—we weren't at a dead stop like I had supposed. Rather, God blessed us, and we progressed in unexpected ways.

Dennis was finally ready to swim, and he progressed from level one to level five before the season ended. A year after he learned to swim, he joined a local swim team for a couple of seasons. Three years later, when he was in high school, he was a lifeguard and taught swimming lessons.

Although a transplant couldn't happen as soon as we'd hoped it would, we received help with better dialysis and an early entrance into the transplant process. We received as much as possible as soon as possible.

When we understand God meets us where we are during our waiting periods, it's easier for us to quiet our cries and trust Him. We can play in the water, knowing that as soon as all aspects are ready, He will take the next step to help us move forward.

Even as we wait, one way God gives us as much as He can is by sending help into our lives to ease our burdens, which is what he did for us.

CHAPTER 8

SERVING AS JESUS SERVED

*"The Son of man came not to be
ministered unto, but to minister . . ."*

(Matthew 20:28)

I wound my way through the Uinta Mountain meadow a short distance from camp. July sun warmed my hair, a sharp contrast to the confusion swirling inside. I was in my early twenties and wanted to know what direction I should take for my future, especially since the prospects of marriage evaded me. I wanted to settle down and raise a family, but until it happened, I didn't want to let life pass by with me just waiting. Should I go back to college and finish my degree? Should I stay working as a secretary and hope I'd meet someone? Should I move and change my social setting?

I knelt in the dirt. The chirping of the birds, along with the scent of sagebrush and wildflowers, faded from my consciousness as I poured out my heart to God. No answer came. I read my scriptures, wrote in my journal, and took a nap. When I awoke, I turned to my scriptures again. "For behold, this is my work and my glory—to bring to pass the immortality and eternal life of man" (Moses 1:39).

Stunned, I read the verse again. The cloud in my mind parted, and light shone through. I had my answer, only it wasn't the answer I'd expected.

God's entire purpose—everything He does—is to serve others. That's what He wanted me to do. Lift and serve and bring others to Him. He didn't reveal the immediate course of action for me to take. That information came over the years, bit by bit and day by day, as I lived and prayed. Instead, on that sunny afternoon, He gave me a grounding principle to incorporate into every decision I would make. Include service in my life.

I did just that as I finished college, pursued a career, and married. With a life built on the principle of self-reliance, I was free to serve others. The ironic thing is that for people to serve, others need to accept the gift of being served. I never wanted to be on the receiving end, but that is exactly where I landed during the year of 2011.

It was one thing to accept prayers and Papa Murphy's Pizza left on my doorstep. It was another to accept help for the every-day tasks I should do, such as maintaining my house and yard. But what I should do, didn't matter. No matter how hard I tried, I couldn't get it done. Family and neighbors came to the rescue.

The evening of Martin's first dialysis treatment, I emailed our extended family with an update. Early the next morning, my brother Neil's wife, Callie, wrote back. "Is there anything I can do for you, you know, help clean your house, make you some dinner, or just be there whenever you need me? Let me know. I love you."

Her concern touched my heart and warmed my morning—just as the other sincere, yet generic, offers of help I received.

An hour later she sent another reply, "I have decided that I am going to come every Friday and clean your house." She wanted to know what time to arrive. She also asked me to identify two sections of my house she could clean because she didn't have time to clean everything.

Embarrassed, I delayed my reply until evening, "You are a gem! Thank you for your offer. But it's such a long drive with gas prices soaring! We'll be okay."

Two hours later, I received her reply. "My car gets great gas mileage, and a 'long drive' is relative. I really want to do this."

How could I ask her to drive forty-five minutes one way to clean my house? I didn't want to accept her help. To be a project. Life wasn't so bad that I required help. The dishes got done even if the floor didn't get swept and mopped. We were surviving.

I didn't respond.

A couple of days later, she talked to me on the phone. "I really want to help, but I'm not going to keep bugging you. Let me know if you change your mind."

My emotions battled with reason. We were doing okay, I insisted. We survived even if the house wasn't spotless. Not that I couldn't clean or that my kids couldn't help. We could do it—at least when not too overwhelmed to think about it and actually pick up the broom to sweep. Most days I roamed around the house in a daze. I gazed out the window at the growing mountain of weeds. I looked at the dirt covering the kitchen floor. Maybe we weren't surviving as well as I pretended.

I swallowed my pride and accepted her offer.

On Friday, Callie walked through the front door, carrying her own cleaning supplies. She brushed her hair out of her face.

"How are you doing?" she asked and crossed the room to give me a hug.

"Hanging in there." I sat on the couch by the front window. Sun filled the room and highlighted dust on the end table. "I don't know how to thank you for coming."

"That's what family's for," she said and went back to her car to bring in her favorite vacuum. When she left, the house smelled different—clean and fresh. When was the last time I had dusted? I couldn't remember. She lifted a burden I didn't even realize was weighing me down, stripping serenity.

Callie cleaned for me until Katie moved home from college and could help. My love for her grew and grew. Each time she came, I hugged her tightly and said thank you. I didn't know what else I could do to show her my gratitude. By cleaning my house, she exemplified Christ, who always "went about doing good" (Acts 10:38). Each time she came, the clouds parted over my mountain meadow and let the light of Christ warm my soul. Through her actions, I knew Him better. As Elder M. Russell Ballard said, "Service opens a window by which we understand the life and ministry of Christ. He came to serve" ("Precious Gifts from God," 10).

Service isn't always about the receiver. It is also about what happens to the giver when the receiver accepts the help. We learned this profoundly.

Late in the summer, a member of the bishopric approached Martin. "What can we do to help your family?"

"We don't need anything," Martin said. "The ward has already been so kind."

A week never went by without a ward member dropping off flowers, buying Martin his favorite milkshake, or driving the kids on errands. How could we ask for more?

"I get that," the counselor said. "But the ward is having a day of service. We'd like to add your family to our list. What can we do?"

"Really, our family can help with whatever we need."

"Martin," his voice deepened with authority. "We know you have family who can help. But the ward members need to serve you, and you need to let them."

Humbled once again, we acquiesced. Early in September, several brothers and sisters showed up and tackled a domestic yard that resembled a free-form mountain meadow complete with random weeds growing wherever they felt like growing. My ward family weeded the vast flower beds, fixed sprinklers, and repaired the rain gutter. They turned our overgrown yard into a landscape worthy of a home show if not an English manor.

Reflecting on this experience, I realized Christ accepted service. He accepted fish and bread from a boy before the miracle to feed five thousand. He allowed Mary to anoint His feet with oil. He rode on a borrowed donkey for His triumphal entry into Jerusalem. He asked to use a family's upper room for the Last Supper.

The Lord said "yes" to every individual who offered to serve Him then, and He does so now. When we say yes, we mirror the Savior. As we serve, we love the person we are serving more and become more committed to the cause we are giving to. That is one reason the Lord asks us to serve in callings. It deepens our dedication to Him and His church.

My family could have managed without our neighbors' time and effort. We washed the dishes and picked up the clutter. Weeding wasn't essential to our ability to live. But, just as the bishopric member told us, the ward needed to serve. As we humbly accepted their gifts of love, they loved the Savior more, and we did too.

Cleaning and weeding helped. But there were so many other duties I had no energy to tackle. My mother-in-law came to my rescue when she addressed a pressing task I'd been procrastinating for months.

Toward the close of 2010, Brian had completed every requirement for his Eagle Scout. It was a prestigious time to receive that rank since it was the one hundredth anniversary of the year the United States brought Scouting to our country. His Eagle badge contained the commemorative date.

We waited to plan his court of honor until the national board approved the rank advancement. By the time that happened, Martin's health problems eclipsed anything else. I put it off, knowing it needed to happen but without the strength to make it so.

"Michelle," my mother-in-law, Arda Jean, said in early June. "When is Brian's Eagle Court of Honor?"

"Oh, I don't know," I said. Guilt flooded my body. He'd earned it over eight months ago.

"It'd be nice to do it this summer when everyone is in town for the family reunion." She was the proud grandmother of several grandsons who were Eagle Scouts. Each one, including my two older boys, had received a huge celebration in his honor. The thought of planning a program, getting commendation letters, sending invitations, and all the other traditional details weighed me down further than I already was.

"I know." I sighed. "I need to do it."

"It just needs to happen,"

I looked at her. "I'll try."

"Let me do it." Arda Jean assured me that Brian's cousins could help; they needed something to do while they stayed with her that summer.

At first, I resisted. It was the job of Brian's mother to plan it for her son. But my mother-in-law was right. It just had to happen. Brian needed the boost. He needed to celebrate the good in his life, to take a break from the worry that permeated his heart. Grateful, and a little embarrassed, I accepted her offer.

The court of honor turned out just like I wanted it. Arda Jean consulted me often and ensured I approved of the program and arrangements. For myself, I retained the job of making his slide show. The hours spent scanning pictures, finding the right music, and arranging the slide show reminded me that life is good. The date of the ceremony book-ended our family reunion and made it possible for Brian's favorite cousins to attend and honor him.

"Thank you," I said to my mother-in-law after it was over.

She gave me a big hug.

Her efforts rescued me. She liberated me from guilt and worry. She gave Brian a much-needed emotional and mental embrace. Her love saved us both.

Service does that. Service is redemptive. Elder D. Todd Christofferson explained, "While the most important aspects of redemption have to do with repentance and forgiveness, there is a very significant temporal aspect as well" ("Redemption," 110). Jesus Christ's mission on earth extended beyond the atonement and resurrection. The scriptures teach us that "the Son of man came not to be ministered unto, but to minister . . ." (Matthew 20:28).

Everywhere Christ went, He not only lifted the spiritual burdens of those around Him, He also lifted their temporal burdens. We can mirror the Savior as we ". . . go about doing good in the redemptive pattern of the Master. This kind of redemptive work means helping people with their problems" (Christofferson, 110).

Even when we struggle, we can follow the Savior's example to help others. Martin had that opportunity during his sick days. In mid-June, we received an expected, dreaded call.

"Rolf passed this morning."

"We'll head right over to Jean's," said Martin without hesitating.

We stopped at a grocery store before we left for Ogden, Utah. Martin wanted to buy his sister something to comfort her, to let her know he loved her and understood her pain.

"Let's get a watermelon," he said. "It's Jean's favorite. Growing up, mom and dad bought her one every year on her birthday, even though it was out of season in February. I want to take her one now."

Memories of Rolf and sorrow for Jean filled our conversation during the thirty-minute drive. We talked about what to do, how to help, and what to say. Martin, more than any other family member, including their parents, understood his sister's grief. He'd been there. He knew.

We arrived at her house and climbed the stairs with heavy steps. Jean threw her arms around her younger brother.

"Thank you for coming. You know what it's like."

Martin held her tight and stroked her hair. "I know," he said. "It is awful. I'm so sorry you have to go through this."

"I'm in your club now," Jean attempted a laugh that failed. "It's an awful club to be in."

Martin took the watermelon from me and gave it to his sister.

"Watermelon," Jean said with a smile this time. "It's my favorite."

We stayed the rest of the day with Jean, listened to her, cried with her, loved her. Nearly every day for the next week, Martin and I drove to her house after dialysis.

She wanted help writing an obituary, so Martin brain-stormed ideas with her, drawing upon his prior knowledge of writing Sherri's obituary. She asked Martin to design the funeral program, complete with a full-color collage of family pictures. Martin took scanned photos from Jean and created a touching slide show for the viewing. He gathered memorabilia and set up a display table near the slide show during the services.

The little things he did comforted Jean. But perhaps the biggest service he provided was hope for the future, hope that through the power of the Savior's atonement, life would get better one day. Martin stood as living proof that God is merciful. He'd lost his wife, and God blessed him with healing, recovery, and a new life. He would do it for Jean, too, in a way unique to her but good.

Martin didn't have a lot of energy to assist others during his illness. He gave what he had when he could. Even when we are low, we can always find ways to serve others. That's what the Savior did. During His final hours, Jesus comforted the thief who hung next to him. He asked His servant John to take care of His mother. He thought about others.

As Martin served his sister, his own burdens lightened. His testimony of God's plan of salvation and eternal families was strengthened, and with power, he declared that God is compassionate and kind. His words and actions reminded both him and me that God was aware of him too. Service changed Martin, and it changed me.

Service changes all of us; it saves us. President Thomas S. Monson said, ". . . unless we lose ourselves in service to others, there is little purpose to our own lives. Those who live only for themselves eventually shrivel up and figuratively lose their lives, while those who lose themselves in service to others grow and flourish—and in effect save their lives" ("What Have I Done for Someone Today?," 85). Little did I realize, on that Uinta mountain meadow all those years ago, what a powerful, saving concept God taught me.

The gifts of love from our ward and family helped rescue us emotionally. Accepting those small acts of service was one thing. Asking for someone to be a donor—to provide such a tremendous sacrifice on Martin's behalf—was an entirely different matter. The very idea of making that request filled Martin with agony.

CHAPTER 9

WE NEED CHRIST IN EVERY ASPECT OF LIFE

"And since man had fallen he could not merit anything of himself; but the sufferings and death of Christ atone for their sins."

(Alma 22:14)

I don't know about you, but when I'm dealing with a two- or three-year-old toddler, I often hear, "Do it by myself," or "Me do it." Once a growing toddler utters that phrase, no amount of coaxing can change the child's mind. Even if the task is far beyond the little one's ability, he or she will try and try and try. Failure results in tears and frustration and maybe even a tantrum.

Sometimes I feel just like the three-year-old when dealing with life. I grit my teeth, square my shoulders, and announce, "I can do this," even when I can't. Sometimes my failure to succeed results in tears and frustration and even a tantrum now and then. Sometimes, regardless of the failure, I persist in trying and end up with the sense of going it alone, doing it alone, striving alone day after day after day. Alone.

That's not an accurate picture. Even when we don't recognize God's hand in our lives, He sustains us more than we realize, just like dialysis did a lot more than either Martin or I recognized. During the first few months of the ghastly treatment, my entire focus was Martin's unfavorable health, and the poor job dialysis did in making him feel better.

About the time Dr. Conrad suggested a switch to PD, Martin expressed his doubt that dialysis was doing much. In April when he was first hooked up to the machine, it all happened so fast, too fast to analyze the information and make an informed decision. As the days, weeks, and months wore on, we wondered if he needed dialysis because he still had some residual kidney function. Dr. Conrad assured Martin that he could safely skip treatments for a week and see how he did. After the trial run, they could evaluate his health and decide about future treatments.

Perfect timing. Martin's extended family had a reunion for a week at a family camp on the west side of Mount Timpanogos. Dialysis would have required a one-hour round-trip drive to the Provo, Utah, clinic, along with four hours of treatment. It would be nicer if he didn't have to leave the camp three times during the gathering.

Aspen Grove Family Camp was the ideal place for the trial. The clean mountain air carried the fresh scent of pine. Birds chirped and darted back and forth as they played with each other. Squirrels and chipmunks scurried across the trails. Laughter and energetic conversation floated in the air everywhere we went.

The camp staff cooked all the meals. They provided daytime activities for the children and youth, which included arts and crafts, hiking, swimming, and archery. Our kids relaxed and had fun with their cousins. Smiles, jokes, and exciting activities erased the strain of living in an uneasy house.

The camp offered adult classes and activities, too. I attended a few, but most of the time I relaxed with the family. Tension eased out of my jaw, neck, and shoulders as the week progressed. Martin slept most of the time. He attended the daily family devotionals and returned to the bedroom as soon as they concluded. After using a lathe to turn a wooden pen, he took a nap. Sleep book-ended short, rejuvenating visits with his siblings.

One highlight of staying in the mountains was the array of hiking opportunities. Two thirds of the way through a week without dialysis,

Martin and I took a small hike. Seven years earlier we summited Mt. Timpanogos together. That was impossible this year. Not only because of Martin's health, but snow still covered most of the trail during the last part of June. The trailhead was open though, so we could take a little hike together.

Martin's youngest brother, Glenn, and his wife joined us. Martin set the pace on the rough, rocky trail. We climbed at a labored speed, much slower than Glenn's robust fitness usually carried him up the mountains. It didn't matter because the point was to enjoy nature and each other's company.

The dirt path wove in and out of shady trails, and the sun warmed our bodies more than the simple exertion did. A refreshing breeze fluttered through the quaking aspens. Glenn's energetic voice echoed off the surrounding rocks and cliffs. A mile up the Timpanogos trail we reached the snow fall that still needed to melt after a wet winter.

The two brothers posed for a picture, shoulder to shoulder, both close to six feet six inches tall. Martin's premature gray made a distinctive contrast to Glenn's dark hair. The physical attributes were not the biggest difference between the two. Rather, it was the pallor on Martin's face that his smile couldn't hide and the fatigue that caused his frame to sag. Though pleasant, the hike was taking its toll on Martin.

We turned back as the sun disappeared behind clouds. The breeze whipped up more speed and drew our attention to the mountain horizon on the south. Heavy, black clouds hovered over the peaks that jutted upward. The clouds raced each other, heading north across the sky, right toward us. Sheets of dark streaks stretched down from the clouds and obliterated the sky.

Despite the imminent downpour, we hung back, transfixed by the beauty of the approaching storm. I stopped several times, aimed my camera at the scene, and snapped several pictures, even though my camera would never capture the grandeur of the moment.

"It's almost here." Martin said, his voice full of more excitement and pleasure than I'd heard in a long time.

After switching the camera to video, I directed it toward the southern sky once again.

"Here it comes," said Glenn with glee.

Torrents of rain dumped on us less than a minute later. I shoved my camera out of the weather and turned my face up to greet the refreshing rain. Cold water ran down my eyes and cheeks. Some landed inside my open smile.

The dusty trail changed to mud, and tiny rivulets followed the sloping path. We picked our way down, sheltered off and on by the overhanging bows of the pine trees. Rain muted the sound of our laughter but couldn't dampen the delight in our heart. We made it back to the lodge, safe and invigorated. At least I was invigorated.

Martin was laughing but dragging at the same time. Once he changed his clothes, Martin collapsed on the bed, his energy depleted. He drifted into a more restful sleep than usual, but the sleep didn't restore him.

The toll of no dialysis showed. Although Martin enjoyed the reprieve from his treatments, the small benefit he derived from the blood exchange was missing. He was mentally ready to resume dialysis when we returned home.

The week Martin didn't have dialysis was the week his body tried to do it alone, without help. It didn't work very well. It is a mirror that reminds us we need the help of Jesus Christ, that none of us can go alone. Sister Michelle D. Craig, from the Young Women's General Presidency said, "there is some truth in the realization that *alone* we are not enough. But the good news of the gospel is that with the grace of God, we *are* enough" ("Divine Discontent," 54).

Just like the three-year-old, no matter how much we try to do it by ourselves, no matter how much we think we can do it by ourselves, living without the Lord's help is difficult and draining, just like it was for Martin the week he had no treatments. God's help is a fundamental part of our existence and extends beyond our day-to-day activities into eternity.

It's a plain and simple truth. We cannot save ourselves. We learned this lesson in a profound way the day we went to the hospital for Martin's transplant intake appointment.

The alarm sounded early on the morning of July 6, 2011. Martin rolled over with a groan. I sat up to make my way over to the clock and turn it off. Dizziness engulfed my body, and my stomach revolted.

I fought back the tears. It was transplant intake day, the day we'd prayed would come for three months, and I was sick with either food poisoning or a stomach bug.

"Martin, I'm not sure I can go. I'm sick, and I might throw up. I don't know if I'm contagious, but . . ." My silent thoughts pled with him to understand, to suggest that it would be fine if one of our children went in my place. Maybe Katie or William? They could take lots of notes.

He rubbed his forehead and his shoulders slumped. Dismay filled his eyes. "Maybe you could take some Pepto Bismol?" he said.

The desperate tone of his voice echoed my own anxious thoughts. He was right. The meetings were too important. It was at this meeting that we'd meet the transplant team of doctors, surgeons, nutritionists, and pharmacists. We needed two sets of ears listening to the instructions, sorting, sifting, and making sense of what they were saying.

But I could barely stand, let alone walk. How would I do it? The thought of eating sent waves of nausea coursing through my entire system. I was afraid that if I wasn't running to the nearest restroom in search of a toilet, I'd be sitting in the corner of the room, too sick to care, and way too sick to understand what they said.

As his wife, though, I had to be there. I couldn't turn this over to anyone else. No one else cared as much as I did, for no one else loved him as I did. They wouldn't take notes like I would and wouldn't know what questions they should ask. I wanted the answers directly, unfiltered, and discussed until I was satisfied with the answers. While my kids loved their father, they didn't have the same vested interest, the same knowledge of Martin's condition, the same bond of love. I had to be with Martin, next to him, united with him. Regardless of how I felt, I couldn't miss it. I just couldn't.

"You're right. I'll come."

I stumbled around the house and collected items we needed to take, a notebook and pens, photo I.D., doctors' contact info, dates of Martin's recent surgeries. And a bottle of Pepto-Bismol with a spoon.

I staggered into the shower and leaned against the walls to steady my legs while I soaped and rinsed my body. The makeup I put on did little to hide the chalky white face that stared back from the mirror.

It couldn't be helped. I pushed the cosmetics bag onto the counter, forced a smile, and greeted my husband, ready to go.

The huge parking lot at Intermountain Medical Center in Murray, Utah, contained several empty spaces close to the building because of the early hour, and we both shuffled the short distance into the building. The elevator stopped at level three with a bounce that jolted my sensitive stomach. Around a corner and down a long hallway, we approached the transplant clinic for the first time.

Martin registered at the front desk, and we collapsed on the chairs in the waiting area until a nurse escorted us to an examination room. Martin took the vinyl seat that gave the medical staff easier access to him. I dropped into an uncomfortable chair without armrests next to him.

The nurse tugged a regular-sized cuff over Martin's right arm. It was snug even before she tightened the Velcro straps. Martin rested his feet on the floor and waited while the automatic machine inflated and deflated the cuff. His blood pressure was way too high. She tried again.

"Still high." She scribbled the readings on the chart, turned to leave, and paused at the door. "In a few minutes, the lead transplant nephrologist will come and give you an exam." With that, she departed and left us alone.

The time advanced in silence, minute by minute. Martin and I both rested our heads against the wall while we waited. I battled nausea and my thoughts. In my anxious distress, warning bells rang. High blood pressure is a problem for kidneys. It could rule out a transplant, give them a reason to deny Martin's request.

I shifted on my chair, crossed and uncrossed my legs, stood and walked across the room to stretch, and slumped back into the chair again. Queasiness rumbled through my stomach and made me more nervous. "Please, Heavenly Father," I prayed, "please make it be okay. Please. We need this so badly."

The door opened. An older man with a slight build, wearing a white lab coat, entered. The usual pair of stethoscopes hung around his neck. Here was the man with the power to wield a yes or no verdict. My nerves tightened around my rumbling stomach and added to the queasiness.

He shook Martin's hand. "I'm one of the nephrologists." His humble introduction said nothing about him being the lead doctor. "Later you'll meet with the surgeons and others, but I get you first." His tone was light-hearted, and I noticed the wrinkles in his face lifted with his smile. His easy-going manner relieved some of my mental pressure.

He reviewed the charts and came right to the point in a kind but business-like tone. "Do you have problems with high blood pressure?"

"Not usually. On dialysis it's been worse."

"You're a big guy. I'll bet the high reading was a problem with the automatic machine. They're never as accurate. And that cuff? Too small to be accurate." He wanted to take it himself, old-school style, with his own stethoscope resting on Martin's arm.

A silent, tentative sigh escaped from my heart. Maybe it wasn't as bad as I feared. Maybe.

The doctor found a bigger cuff attached to a manual squeeze pump and adjusted it over Martin's bicep. He removed the stethoscope from around his neck and placed it on Martin's arm. With quick, sure movements, he inflated the cuff and slowly released the pressure.

"Just as I thought," he said when he finished. "It was the cuff. You don't have high blood pressure."

Good news. My shoulders relaxed while the physician continued his examination. He asked Martin questions about his health, lifestyle habits, and problems that caused the kidneys to fail. I jotted down notes where I could, capturing his muttered comments. Was he was talking to himself or to Martin or both? It didn't matter. Ignoring my muddled brain, I wrote as fast as I could. Detailed notes were the best assurance we had of understanding the nuances later.

"Never smoked. Good blood pressure. Weight is fine. No genetic problems that could interfere. Hmm. Good candidate. I will transplant you."

It surprised us to hear such a blunt assessment. All other medical personnel couched their comments in terms of the decision being made by a committee. As program director, he talked as if it was his program. With his blessing, we believed it would happen.

"Everything looks great. You're young and otherwise healthy. You'll do well with transplant."

I uttered a quick, silent prayer. "Thank you, Heavenly Father. Thank you." I looked at Martin. The relief I felt shown in his eyes. More meetings and many tests had to happen before they committed to a transplant. We knew that. Yet, at this moment, we knew we'd just crossed a major hurdle.

The day progressed, and my stomach recovered bit by bit. Although I avoided any mad dashes to the nearest restroom, my mind remained cloudy. Names and faces blurred. The details and information blended. At least I had notes to refer to.

My mind grasped several important pieces of information. Kidneys retrieved from deceased donors differ from living donor kidneys. The organs transplanted from a deceased donor lasted an average of ten years. These came from the national transplant list, and the average waiting time was two years. A living donor's kidney lasts an average of fifteen years, and transplant could happen as fast as we found a compatible donor. A longer lasting kidney and a faster transplant time. Of course, we hoped for a living donor.

"You can thank your parents for having so many kids," one doctor said when he discovered Martin was one of eight. "Siblings make better matches."

Seven siblings. It seemed inevitable that he'd find a living donor and find one soon. Already many of Martin's siblings had volunteered to sacrifice one of their kidneys for him.

"What do you think?" I asked Martin on the way home. The late afternoon sun cast long shadows from the cars on the freeway. We'd been at the hospital all day. It was a lot to take in, and the thirty-minute ride gave us an opportunity to talk before greeting the chaos of a family we had left unattended for several hours.

"I'm grateful I have seven brothers and sisters."

"Me, too."

"But it's humbling. I'm asking for something huge. This isn't a small deal."

"I know," I said, and reached for his hand. "But it's the best way."

"I know. And it's what we've prayed for and what we want. But still . . ." We drove in silence for a few miles before he continued. "Today it hit me just what we're asking one of my brothers or sisters to do. It's a huge sacrifice on their part. Just for me."

He was right. A living donor had to undergo major surgery. With advanced technology, most procedures were outpatient and required only one to two days in the hospital. Not a transplant. The donor could stay in the hospital up to a week. Any surgery was risky, especially major surgery. The chances were low, but still existed, that someone could die during the operation.

In addition, a donor would give up a working organ. The physicians told us donors have a harder time right after surgery than recipients. It was like a donor would go through temporary kidney failure while the body adapted.

Once home, it would take six weeks to recover. Six weeks of suffering and misery, of missing work and other activities, of disrupting normal daily life. Six weeks.

And we were going to ask one of Martin's dear family members to sacrifice in that manner so Martin could live a better life.

How could he ask that of someone? It didn't seem fair. But without it, Martin's life span would decrease by several years.

As we talked, I saw an immediate mirror to our Savior. Just as someone had to sacrifice to save Martin, the Savior sacrificed to save all of us. Without His atonement, we would die physically, spiritually, eternally.

We prayed the donor's life would be spared and only temporarily interrupted, and the statistics assured us it would be so. But Christ's life wasn't spared. Not only did He die, but before His crucifixion, He suffered in Gethsemane beyond anything we can ever imagine. The scriptures tell us that our physical bodies could not have survived the intense pain and pressure the Savior suffered.

Jesus did it so we could have a better life in mortality and a glorious life in the eternities. His sacrifice wasn't fair. But we need it. Because of our sins and imperfections—our mortality—it's impossible for us to be in the presence of God without help. As Alma said, "since man had fallen he could not merit anything of himself; but the sufferings and death of Christ atone for their sins" (Alma 22:14). We cannot do it alone no matter how hard we try. Without Jesus Christ, we would be lost forever and in the grasp of "that awful monster the devil" (2 Nephi 9:19).

Contemplating the sacrifice we were going to ask someone else to make for Martin, helped me understand our Redeemer's sacrifice better. Likewise, the requirements to be a donor mirrors the Savior, in a way I'd never expected.

CHAPTER 10

Jesus Had to Be Both Mortal and Immortal

*"The Father, because he was conceived by the
power of God; and the Son, because of the flesh;
thus becoming the Father and Son."*

(Mosiah 15:3)

Six months before I met Martin, I sat on a train speeding from Manhattan toward White Plains, New York. I was spending three weeks back East for my company. Across from me sat two coworkers who asked me an important question.

"What's the main difference between your church and other Christian churches?"

How should I answer? Several options raced through my mind. I wanted to get it right. I should start with Jesus Christ.

"Well, we believe that Jesus Christ is the literal son of our Heavenly Father."

Confusion reigned on their faces. "So you don't believe in the Immaculate Conception?"

"Well, we believe Heavenly Father is Christ's literal father and Mary is His literal mother." I continued and explained why Christ had to be both mortal and immortal. After I'd answered all their questions, I wasn't sure how much they understood of this doctrine that is central to The Church of Jesus Christ of Latter-day Saints. If I'd understood organ donation back then, I could have answered their questions much better.

Though Martin agonized over the need to ask another person to lay his or her life on the line to save his, he never had to approach anyone. Family members and friends came from everywhere, volunteering to donate. Martin's siblings, my sister, my sister-in-law, ward members, friends, and the list went on.

The outpouring of love from all who volunteered humbled us. So many people loved Martin and our family enough to seek us out. I had no idea what to say to everyone. I tried to say thank you, but words didn't cover it. How do you thank people who are willing to risk their lives to save your husband?

The day after the intake, we gathered at the home of Martin's parents for a family barbecue. One of Martin's older sisters, Jolene, carried a tray of food to the picnic table. Her shoulder length hair fell forward as she bent her lean six-foot frame toward the table. She picked up a plate and loaded it with a large serving of the green salad and tiny portions of the picnic food. She brought her food to a chair next to Martin and sat down to hear the news.

All eyes were on him. Glenn, Martin's youngest brother, grabbed a chair and dragged it across the deck. Had it only been two weeks since the mountain downpour drenched us? I could have sworn at least a year had passed.

Martin shook his head and tried to speak. Nothing came out. He cleared his throat and tried again. "Thank you all, so much. It's really humbling for me to see your love. I hate asking this." Martin paused, unable to continue for a moment.

Jolene reached over to squeeze his hand. She, Glenn, and others had already expressed an interest in donating a kidney for him.

Martin told them about the information we gathered the day before. He explained one of the initial requirements for a donor is that the person has nearly flawless health. The medical team refused to put a donor's life at risk; therefore, each volunteer had to be physically strong and healthy. Martin rattled off several requirements based on their criteria.

Donors had to be at a healthy weight. They couldn't have diabetes, high blood pressure, cancer, hepatitis, or other serious health problems. They couldn't have had previous damage to either kidney, which ruled out anyone who'd ever had kidney stones. Donors had to be emotionally stable and mentally capable of dealing with such a difficult surgery and recovery.

Martin assured them that because donors met such stringent requirements, the outlook for their long-term health was excellent. To date, none of their donors had suffered any health problems due to transplant in the succeeding years.

"The first meeting will be a prescreen interview, probably over the phone," he said. "They'll ask you a lot of questions to ensure you are healthy enough to give up an organ."

I looked around at Martin's siblings. Because willingness to donate wasn't enough, Martin didn't want to ask anyone directly. He preferred to let them to evaluate their health and come to him on their own.

"One more thing. No one has to cover this financially. My insurance will take care of it. Think about it, and if you're interested, let me know," Martin said. "I'll get you the information."

Glenn and Jolene volunteered immediately, along with some others. Martin shook his head softly, and tears welled in his eyes. He swallowed hard and let out a deep breath.

"The tests are so expensive that they only want to test two people at first," Martin said. "Once the tests progress far enough, they'll narrow it down to one. When one volunteer is eliminated, another can step in until they get a match."

Tears fell down my face unheeded. My overwrought mind released a measure of tension that had held it captive for months. What could I say to Martin's siblings? I loved them so much. They were willing to submit to an extensive surgery with a grueling recovery and put their own lives on hold to save the life of their brother. Because of their love and generosity, my family could have a more normal life.

Cancer, diabetes, and other health problems eliminated some. Others lived too far away to complete the testing. In the end, Jolene and Glenn remained the only siblings able to proceed.

I was so happy, so grateful. My inadequate prayers filled my soul with reverence and love. Love for Jolene. Love for Glenn. Love for all his siblings. Love for Heavenly Father and Jesus.

Over the next couple of days, Martin gave both Glenn and Jolene the contact information for Vicki, his transplant coordinator, a registered nurse trained in the details of transplant. She coordinated all the details for Martin, his donor, and medical staff on the team. If we had any questions, we contacted her.

A few days later, the phone rang, and Martin answered it.

"Hi Martin. It's Jolene."

He turned the phone outward from his ear, and I hovered near to hear the conversation.

"I'm so sorry," she said. Her voice was soft with disappointment. "I called and talked to Vicki for the prescreen interview. We didn't get very far before she told me I couldn't do it."

My heart sank. Why? Jolene seemed so healthy. She was diligent about keeping weight down. She had been healthy enough to serve a couples' mission in a third-world country. Why her?

"Remember the pulmonary embolism I had fifteen years ago?" Jolene said, referring to the time she nearly died when a blood clot hit her lungs. "Well, as soon as Vicki heard about it, the interview was over. She didn't even ask me about anything else." Vicki had explained the likelihood of another clot was too great, and they weren't willing to take the risk.

"It's all right," Martin said. "Thank you for trying. I really appreciate it."

"I'm so sorry. I'll keep praying for you. And I'll pray for Glenn. He's still being screened, right?"

"Yes. He is."

"He's really healthy," Jolene said. "I'm sure he'll be able to donate."

Martin hung up the phone, and we stared at each other. Now what?

My heart sank. Of course, we wouldn't want anything to happen to Jolene. We wouldn't want her to jeopardize her life. No way. But the reality was that when she got eliminated, we only had one candidate left. One out of seven. The disappointment was a bitter pill to swallow.

I had no idea it would be so difficult to find a person to save my husband.

The conditions necessary for a person to donate a major organ mirror our Redeemer's ability to perform the atonement. Just as an unhealthy donor could not make the sacrifice to save Martin, mortal man cannot redeem mankind from both spiritual and physical death. Mortal man is simply not capable.

The only way for us to be redeemed from both our sins and our mortality is through a sacrifice that only a God had the capability to perform. The sacrifice had to cover everything from the beginning of time to the end. As Amulek said, "there can be nothing which is short of an infinite atonement which will suffice for the sins of the world" (Alma 34:12). If Jesus Christ wasn't a God, He wouldn't have had the capability of making the sacrifice.

Jesus Christ had to be flawless to pay for the sins of all eternity. He had to face temptation, resist it, and remain one hundred percent sinless and flawless. He also had to have the power over life and death. He had to give up his life and take it back again so that "the grave [would] deliver up its captive bodies" (2 Nephi 9:12). Without the resurrection, we would remain trapped in Satan's grasp.

Only a God could accomplish these things. Because He was God, Jesus could pay the price for all sins and troubles in the world. Because He was God, Jesus Christ could bring about our resurrection.

It is easy for me to understand the need for Jesus Christ to be a God. It makes sense. But sometimes the question might arise of why He had to be a mortal too. Since God is all powerful, why couldn't He just pay for our sins and bring about the resurrection?

The other organ donor requirements helped make sense of why Christ had to be mortal.

With Jolene's news, Martin and I took a step back and analyzed the situation. It wasn't the end of the world. We still had hope because Glenn still moved forward. I calmed my mind and focused my hopes on Martin's brother.

Because siblings share DNA from the same set of parents, it's easier to get a match from a brother or sister. Every individual has a unique composite that makes up their organs. For a person to be an adequate match, he or she must share enough of the same blood type, proteins, antibodies, and tissue. If Martin received a kidney not compatible with his own, his immune system would develop antibodies that would reject the kidney. Brothers and sisters share more of the same elements than anyone else, which is why they are such excellent matches.

Martin only had one sibling left in the process. Surely, he would be able to donate. Surely, he'd be a match. Surely, we could get this done quickly, maybe before the holidays.

But why leave only one person in the queue when the doctors would allow two people to be working toward donation? If the unthinkable happened and Glenn ended up unable to donate, the other person could have completed many preliminary tests. If we waited to know for certain about Glenn, we could lose valuable time that would steal from Martin's life.

The heavy question loomed. Who could he ask?

A tiny nugget started at the back of my mind. What about me? I hesitated. Would it be wise to have both parents undergo surgery at the same time? Who would take care of Martin? Who would run the household while Martin recovered? Who would comfort and stabilize a family already in upheaval?

Not to mention the fact that all medical procedures terrified me. I had fainted more than once when blood was involved. I tamped down the thought of being tested.

What about one of our children? Three of them, William, Adam, and Katie, were old enough, since they were older than eighteen. But they were so young and had many things going on in their lives.

William was looking for a new job. Not a good idea to tell a prospective employer you would need six weeks off work right after you started.

Adam and his wife had discussed it, and he had volunteered. But he was still in college. We didn't know when they would actually schedule the surgeries. We hoped it would be in November or December, but we didn't know. That meant Adam would have to quit school for the upcoming semester without a guarantee that surgery would take place during that time. It might be pushed to next semester. In that case, Adam would forfeit an entire year of school, a year of preparing for a career to support his family. All the time would be wasted.

The same complications arose with Katie. She was still in college. Both Adam and Katie needed to finish their schooling on schedule.

Someone else? While Martin preferred a member of the family, there was the option of someone else. The success of the deceased donor program gave plenty of evidence that unrelated donors could be an adequate match. Therefore, a living, non-related donor might be a possibility.

In understanding the need for donors to match recipients, I gained a deeper appreciation for the need that Jesus had to be mortal too. The Apostle Paul said, "Wherefore in all things it behoved him to be made like unto his brethren, . . . to make reconciliation for the sins of the people" (Hebrews 2:17). A different translation of the same scripture explains it this way, "he had to be made like them, fully human in every way" (Hebrews 2:17, NIV).

Justice requires payment to satisfy a broken law. Because we are fallen, we can't make all the necessary payments ourselves. Heavenly Father couldn't pay the price because He is an exalted being and "cannot look upon sin with the least degree of allowance" (D&C 1:31). Without the Atonement of Jesus Christ, Heavenly Father couldn't even be in our presence, let alone assume the burden of our sins. The price has to be paid by a mortal who can experience what mortals go through.

Paying for our sins isn't the only reason Jesus had to be mortal. He had to die physically in order to be resurrected and break the "bands of death" (Mosiah 15:9). A God could not die. A God could not be sacrificed. Only a mortal could. President Russell M. Nelson said, "He was the only one who could voluntarily lay down His life and take it up again" ("His Mission and Ministry," 5).

Jesus Christ had to be God so He could make the sacrifice, and He had to be mortal to satisfy the demands of justice. He had to have both the characteristics of God the Father and a mortal son. This is what Abinadi meant when he said that Jesus is "The Father, because he was conceived by the power of God; and the Son, because of the flesh; thus becoming the Father and Son" (Mosiah 15:3).

This aspect of His divine Sonship is a mirror to that of an organ donor who has to be both capable of donating and of providing an adequate match for the recipient.

That was the dilemma. Who would be capable and an adequate match? We wouldn't know the answer until another person completed initial testing. With no way of knowing, we had to act on faith and make a choice.

On a Sunday evening in August, Martin and I gathered with our six children and one daughter-in-law for a family council. We prayed together and sought God's will. Martin explained the situation and asked for their honest input and assessment. William, Adam, and Katie all volunteered, as we knew they would.

The idea that I should be tested surfaced again and wouldn't be squelched. I couldn't keep quiet. It scared me to death, but something pushed me forward.

"What about me?" I asked at our family council. "I can do it."

Martin resisted. He'd already lost one wife and the mother of his children. He didn't want to take any chances that he and they would lose another. And if the worst happened, and both people died, he didn't want to leave his children orphaned.

I pushed down my own intense fear of surgery and pled my case. "I want to be tested. I'm healthy and can do it. Besides, maybe we should save the younger kids for the future when you need a second transplant. Everyone else who's volunteered will be too old by then."

Martin shook his head.

"You're my husband, and I love you so much. I want to do this," I said.

Again, Martin shook his head. Hurt showed in his eyes. Hurt and fear. He appeared too tired to resist my pressure. "I guess," he said with a sigh. "Anyway, Glenn's my brother. I'm sure he'll be the one to donate."

The next day I ignored anxiety, fueled by a lifetime of terror involving the medical world, and contacted Vicki.

CHAPTER 11

GOD PREPARES US

*"And he received not of the fulness at
first, but continued from grace to grace,
until he received a fulness."*

(D&C 93:13)

— ❧ —

"Ready or not, here I come." As a child, and even as a high-school student on a date, when I heard those words, my stomach tightened a fraction, and my heart sped up. It didn't matter whether I played hide and seek, kick the can, or sardines. I never wanted to get caught. Sometimes I was ready, safe and quiet, hiding in a tree or behind an old shed. At other times, I was not ready. I ran and tried to hide before getting caught.

The panic and terror of running and trying not to get caught were the emotions I lived with each day as I pushed through the battery of tests to qualify me as a kidney donor.

My initial testing proceeded without a snag. I have O-positive blood, the most common blood type; it presented no problems for Martin's A-positive blood. I passed tests that checked my kidney function, blood pressure, blood sugar levels, and weight requirements. I had excellent health. None of the preliminary tests eliminated me. Everything looked good—at least physically.

Emotionally, doubts plagued me. Had I, the one who fainted at the sight of blood, volunteered to be tested, volunteered to let nurses poke my arm and draw blood? What was I thinking? My mind kept running, afraid of getting caught. Had someone asked me forty years earlier if I would entertain the remote possibility of being a kidney donor, of subjecting myself to that intense pain, I'd have laughed. "Not a chance!" A queasy stomach and a vivid imagination kept me away from blood and hospitals. My phobia of medical systems dates back to some of my earliest memories.

When I was about six, I spent a delightful day with my sister and brother at my grandparents' cabin near the Palisades Dam in Idaho. With my two older siblings, I climbed hills, waded through tall grasses, and brushed against bushes and aspen trees. I scrounged in the dirt for empty, white snail shells to use as beads for a necklace. Heaven could not be any better.

My euphoria fled on the drive home. Grandma informed us we all needed to be checked for wood tics. I knew for sure one of those frightening insects had imbedded itself into me. Back at Grandma's, Mom inspected me and declared me clean. Whew; what a relief.

My brother, Neil, didn't fare so well. Dad found one nestled in his stomach. I stared at the brown pest clinging with a tight grip to my little brother's flesh. I watched with horror as Dad took a match and lit it. The room swirled as the burning flame drew nearer and nearer to my brother's tummy.

I awoke on the kitchen floor in the room adjacent to the procedure and saw my mom hovering over me. The room was dark, and I didn't feel well. Neil, on the other hand, was just fine. I sat upright, glad the atrocious business was finished.

My sensitivity to medical drama didn't improve as I grew older, and one day when I was in junior high, I got caught unprepared. I overheard my older sister describe a problem with her friend's brother. An infected foot injury had turned into blood poisoning and progressed to gangrene. A threat of amputation loomed if they didn't get it under control.

The blood dropped from my face and black shadows danced across my vision. I dropped my head to my knees. When the room stopped spinning, I escaped to my bedroom.

Why did I have to hear that gruesome story? That couldn't happen today. Could it? No. I dismissed the story.

A few days later, I awoke with a fever and stayed home from school. Mid-morning, I got off the couch and found Mom in the kitchen.

"Look." I showed her my hand. I had pulled a hangnail the day before in gym, and it had bled a bit. Now red streaks branched upwards from my finger, spread across the back of my hand, and climbed my arm.

"You've got blood poisoning. You need to go to the doctor," she said.

"Stop teasing me. That's not funny." I cried in anguish.

"I'm not teasing."

Visions of green puss and chopped-off limbs filled my mind. I just knew they would have to whack off my hand.

"Mo-om," I wailed as only a fourteen-year-old could when faced with the threat of imminent amputation. I fought the familiar wave of dizziness.

"You'll be fine. We just need to see the doctor."

The physician checked my swollen, oozing finger. He poked and prodded my arm and confirmed the diagnosis of blood poisoning. The infection had spread all the way to my armpit.

"We'll lance her finger and drain the infection." He took a sharp tool and cut into the skin around my fingernail.

Dark spots appeared in front of me, and I teetered on the exam table. The nurse rushed to retrieve a tiny fabric bag of smelling salts and held it to my nose. It only took one whiff of the sharp ammonia, followed by a cough, for the swirling shadows to depart. I sat upright, ready to go home. Instead, the torture continued.

A moment later, the doctor injected a needle full of antibiotics into my opposite arm. Again, blackness swirled. Again, I swayed. Again, smelling salts came to the rescue. Everyone laughed but me.

Who knew a single shot could hurt so much? I didn't think it fair I had to suffer that way. And the smelling salts? Awful. But . . . I spied my five-year-old sister sitting on Mom's lap in the doctor's office, staring at me. I thought it fitting she should share my treatments. After all, what are big sisters for?

"Kim, smell this."

She pulled away, coughing and squealing. We laughed while Mom held her, and the nurse took the tiny bag from my hands. Kim didn't remember the incident when she got older, but my memory of almost passing out from pain remained strong.

We joked about that event and my propensity to faint for years to come. It was funny because it was true. I never could listen to medical horror stories. Even as an adult, I had problems. When I visited someone in the hospital, their "war stories" made me dizzy. More than once I had to leave a relative's sickroom for fresh air before I toppled onto the floor and set off an alarm that would bring the medical staff racing to my aid instead of the sick person's.

I had a definite weakness. If the Lord had left me alone, I never would have been able to face the possibility of donating a kidney. As a child and a teen, I was far from ready.

The Savior, too, didn't come ready for all the things required of Him. Though a God in the premortal life, He condescended to come to earth as a baby. He had to learn how to walk and talk, how to interact with others, how to read the Torah. He started from scratch and had to learn everything, just like you and me.

The Doctrine and Covenants says Jesus "received not of the fulness at the first" (D&C 93:12–14). It is significant that God repeats the exact phrase in three consecutive verses. He wants us to know that, like Christ, we aren't born ready to accomplish all He has in mind for us. We have to grow into it, just as the Savior "continued from grace to grace, until he received a fulness" (D&C 93:13).

God will help us grow, help us get ready for the things we face in life. If we are humble and turn to Him, His "grace is sufficient," and He will "make weak things become strong" (Ether 12:27). We need to turn to Him and be willing to put forth effort. When we do, He can prepare us, even if we don't realize what He is doing.

Unknown to me, God's spirit worked on me as a young adult and moved me to action. I lived with a contradiction. Though I dreaded needles and blood, I had an unquenchable desire to donate blood. I couldn't let it rest.

My first attempt to donate was at Ricks College, which later became BYU Idaho. Everything started out well. I kept my wooziness at bay during the draw. With tottering steps, I moved to the canteen and sat to eat a few snacks while I listened to their instructions:

"If you feel lightheaded, put your head on the table."

My head dropped to the table, and not because they told me to. It lowered of its own volition as the blood drained from my head. The next thing I knew, I lay on a cot staring at the ceiling and the anxious expressions of those helping at the canteen. I had no idea how I got there.

A year later, my work sponsored a blood drive. I determined to take part and be one hundred percent successful. I grabbed a book to distract my mind from the gigantic needle and the pool of red liquid they'd collect.

They cleaned my arm. I read my book. They inserted the needle. I averted my head. Blood trickled through the clear plastic tube and into the bag. I stared, unseeing, at the pages.

Forty-five minutes later, more than twice the time it normally took to finish, an attendant checked me. The blood had stopped flowing. She jiggled the needle to get it moving again. I winced at the pain she inflicted, my book forgotten. An air bubble escaped into the line, contaminated the half-full bag, and rendered it useless.

My head spun and my shoulders slumped as I made my way back to my desk.

Had I done something wrong to stop the flow of blood? Before I'd started, they had told me my blood pressure was too low. I boosted it with caffeine from a cup of hot chocolate and had persisted. Maybe I could try again sometime. Maybe I'd be more successful then.

Two years later, the stake sponsored a blood drive. I wanted to quit running from this persistent fear. I gathered all the courage I could muster and presented myself at the intake desk. The lady screening volunteers turned me away because I had an earache. I pled with them to let me donate. She stuck with the decision.

Once again, I was caught unprepared. Shame burned as I walked away. Why had I even thought I could do this? Maybe some people were not meant to be donors. I must be one of those. Other people could donate. I would find other ways to serve.

I maintained that position for several years. As time passed, though, changes happened bit by bit that I didn't even recognize.

After I married and got pregnant, I faced many needles and blood draws. I learned to rely on the Lord to conquer my fears. I progressed to a point where I wanted to try again.

With more confidence than I had in my earlier years, I drove to the stake center one afternoon. The cool weather outside matched my nervous energy. I'd been running errands all day and had hardly eaten anything. That wasn't unusual. Busy moms don't always eat on schedule.

I passed all the prescreen tests and settled on the red vinyl recliner. Muted sounds of other volunteers echoed in the huge gym. I said a quiet prayer in my heart and asked the Lord to calm my nerves and make the blood flow. The technician brought the huge needle to my inside elbow. I averted my head and held my breath. The sharp jab in my arm made me tighten my neck and shoulders. Once she inserted the needle, I ignored the residual pain and focused on squeezing the ball she placed in my hand. To my surprise, blood streamed out of my arm, through the tubing, and into the bag without a problem. Before long, I finished.

I made my way to the canteen, ate some crackers, drank some juice, and rested. No fainting. Maybe I could do this. Energy disappeared, though, and I plodded my way to the car. During my nephew's Eagle Court of Honor that night, I wanted to find a corner with carpet, curl up on the floor, and sleep until the ceremony ended. Instead, I forced my drained body to sit upright on the cold metal chairs and counted the seconds until I could rest in the car.

Martin looked at me with concern. "Maybe you shouldn't donate blood," he said on the way home.

"I can do it."

"Some people just aren't meant to donate blood. Maybe you're one of them."

I shook my head, determined to do it again. And I did.

I learned to eat a solid lunch before my appointment. I learned to drink plenty of water the day before and the day of the donation. I learned my body would recover and that I could successfully donate blood. That made me feel good, since my O-positive blood was in high demand.

As I persevered, the Lord helped me become successful. President Russell M. Nelson said, "the Lord loves effort, because effort brings rewards that can't come without it" (Jones, "An Especially Noble Calling," 16). Performing this service became easier and enjoyable. By the time I started testing to be an organ donor, needles and the sight of my blood pooling in a bag beside me didn't bother me as much. I even watched when they poked me. Bit by bit, the Lord had prepared me for the current tasks.

God will always lead and shape our lives if we let Him. Elder Ronald A. Rasband taught, "The Lord's hand is guiding you. By 'divine design,' He is in the small details of your life as well as the major milestones" ("By Divine Design," 57).

Yet, even as he is preparing us for the future, He rarely reveals His plans all at once. He knows we can't handle too much too soon. The Lord said, "I say unto you, ye are little children, and ye have not as yet understood how great blessings the Father hath in his own hands and prepared for you; And ye cannot bear all things now; nevertheless, be of good cheer, for I will lead you along" (D&C 78:17–18).

The Savior, Himself, didn't know His mission at the beginning. After acknowledging Christ's helpless state as an infant, President Lorenzo Snow said, "He grew up to manhood, and during His progress it was revealed unto Him who He was, and for what purpose He was in the world" (*Teachings*, 279).

I'm glad that forty years earlier, no one told me I'd be testing to be an organ donor. That would have been like getting caught at hide and seek before I could begin the hunt for a hiding place. Even seven years before Martin's diagnosis, I wasn't ready to know that I'd test to be a donor. My cousin's kidneys failed in 2004. Relief had filled my soul when I learned one of his brothers qualified to donate. That way I didn't even have to consider it.

Now, as I faced the situation, I feared my readiness on an emotional level. However, deep inside, I didn't doubt. The Spirit confirmed I was doing what He wanted. God had prepared me. I was ready.

But readiness doesn't mean desire. Both Martin and I hoped and prayed for Glenn's success. Then complications arose with Glenn's progress.

CHAPTER 12

WE DON'T KNOW
THE WHOLE STORY

*"For my thoughts are not your thoughts,
neither are your ways my ways."*

(Isaiah 55:8)

Years ago, I internalized an important lesson from the story of the Jaredites preparing to venture across the ocean. Sometimes God asks us to make a plan and present it to Him. He asked the Brother of Jared to figure out what to do about light in the vessels (Ether 2:23). The ancient prophet came up with a plan, and the Lord executed it. God touched the stones just like the Brother of Jared asked Him to do.

Figure out what to do and take it to the Lord. I am a master at that lesson. I am always coming up with one plan or another for the Lord and asking Him to carry it out. My problem is that God often—or maybe I could even say most of the time—has a plan different from mine because He knows more than I do.

Moving forward with a transplant for Martin fell into that category. I had a plan to complete everything before the holidays. Get the testing done for Martin's brother. Get the surgery scheduled. Get the transplant taken care of. Be home for Christmas.

It didn't work out that way. My testing proceeded without a hitch. I finished as much as they would allow by mid-September, but Glenn's testing took on a life of its own, and we had to wait for it to finish.

During the slow process, Glenn told us how much he wanted to be the donor. He'd donated blood and donated a car to the kidney foundation. Now all he had left was to donate a kidney, and he'd get all three. Though he joked about the reason he was being tested, we knew his genuine desire came because of love that had grown over the years between the two brothers.

When Glenn was nine, he'd shared a room with his big brother, Martin, who was then eighteen years old. In their room, Martin hung a poster of the Incredible Hulk bursting through a wall. To Glenn's delight, Martin bequeathed the poster on his little brother when Martin left for a mission. What more could a guy have done to secure the devotion of his younger brother for life?

Over the years, the two siblings stayed close. Martin helped Glenn drive to Pennsylvania from Utah when Glenn moved back east, allowing Glenn's wife and little ones to fly out later. During the long drive, the brothers talked via walkie-talkies. Mile after mile with one in a car and the other in a moving van, they shared everything from light conversation to sacred experiences. The drive connected the two men tighter than ever. Fifteen years after that drive, Glenn lived in Utah once again, and the bond they shared grew.

Glenn's testing had odd twists that delayed the process. The hospital couldn't find the blood pressure tests that his doctor had faxed over. Could Glenn please have his doctor refax the tests? A blood pressure test came back too high. Wait. Glenn had taken cold medicine, which artificially elevated it. He needed to retest. The transplant coordinator went on vacation for a week and broke her arm, which kept her from working for a few weeks. More delays.

I did what I could to make things go smoother and spent hours communicating with Vicki to alleviate a bit of red tape for Glenn. But there wasn't a lot I could do. I had to sit back and wait. I had learned earlier, through Martin's testing, that forcing a plan can cause undue grief.

In the middle of the summer, the doctors had drawn several vials of blood from Martin to look for a virus, latent infection, or chronic condition that would interfere with a successful transplant. One wrong blood test could throw the whole thing out the window.

With our hearts and hope on hold, we awaited the results. Let it be good news. Please let it be good news.

Apprehension reigned while we waited. Martin was used to bad news. His first wife's cancer and subsequent death had stripped his innocence. Sherri tried chemotherapy. It failed. She tried stem cell replacement, an experimental therapy for inflammatory breast cancer. It failed. God had other plans for Sherri.

Martin's sister Jean had received bad news. Her husband's failing health revealed liver cancer. The entire family fasted and prayed for Rolf's recovery. God had other plans for him.

Now Martin's health was failing too. All the remedies didn't work as well on him as they did on others.

Bad news after bad news after bad news. We waited for the next shoe of bad news to drop. It had happened in the past. Why would it be any different in the future?

Not knowing the verdict of the labs drove us crazy. We decided to sneak a peek at his patient portal before we met with the doctors. We just had to know. Knowledge is power. Right?

Martin tested negative for hepatitis B. Good. A positive test would disqualify him. He tested negative for hepatitis C. Good. That, too, would disqualify him if it came back positive.

Next? Antibodies for the Epstein-Barr virus, the virus that causes mononucleosis. Positive.

It seemed the next shoe had dropped.

Martin didn't want to live on dialysis, to die on dialysis. He wanted to get better, but it didn't seem to be his lot.

The next week we had a doctor's appointment. The meeting continued on and on, with no mention of the aberrant result. Martin waited with trepidation for the doctor to bring up the fact that he no longer qualified for a transplant. He couldn't stand it any longer.

"What about the Epstein-Barr test? It came back positive."

With a wave, Dr. Conrad allayed our concern. Ninety-five percent of the population tests positive for that antibody. If Martin had been negative, he could have contracted mono should the donor carry positive antibodies. In that case, they'd give Martin an antiviral drug, but since he tested positive for the virus, it was a non-issue.

Relief washed over Martin's face, and his eyes regained a glimmer of hope. We had made judgments based on incomplete information. We didn't know what we didn't know.

This situation is an excellent mirror of our interactions with the Lord. We often approach our problems as if we know all the answers. We believe we have the perfect plan. If God would do it our way, everything would work out. It's as if we are telling God we know what's best. The truth is we don't. We have a limited view and limited knowledge. We don't know what we don't know.

Just like the doctor had more information than we did, God has more understanding than we do. The Lord says, "For my thoughts are not your thoughts, neither are your ways my ways, saith the Lord. For as the heavens are higher than the earth, so are my ways higher than your ways, and my thoughts than your thoughts" (Isaiah 55:8–9).

Knowing that on a logical level can differ from knowing it deep inside your heart and soul. It's hard to internalize it when life is difficult, when we don't have all the answers, when we want the pain to go away. At those times, it is critical we exercise faith in a perfect, loving God. President Dieter F. Uchtdorf said, "Faith . . . means trusting that God loves us perfectly, that everything He does—every blessing He gives and every blessing He, for a time, withholds—is for our eternal happiness" ("Fourth Floor, Last Door," 17).

It is the same in everyday life. When we let go of our own plans and desires in favor of trusting someone with more knowledge, we can have glorious and triumphant experiences. Martin helped me achieve that level of satisfaction in mid-October.

Autumn transformed the Wasatch Mountains. Red and gold speckled the hills above our home in Bountiful. Flocks of geese flew overhead, honking their way south. The crisp smell of fall permeated the air and rejuvenated my body.

On a sunny Saturday in mid-October, Nicole, Dennis, William, and I took Martin hiking on the Mueller Park trail near our home.

"Let's just go as far as I went with the kids yesterday," I said, not wanting Martin to push too hard.

A mile and a half up the canyon, we stopped. Large boulders near the trail provided a great place to sit and snack on string cheese and nuts. The trail overlooked the slopes of the canyon. Fall colors blanketed the valley. We absorbed the beauty while we rested.

"Want to turn back now?" I asked.

"I'm good." Martin pushed forward.

Half an hour later, I checked in again. "Want to go back now?"

"Not yet."

Each time I asked, he wanted to go just a little farther and then a little farther. Deeper into the mountains we hiked, drawing closer and closer to the big rock known by Bountiful residents as Elephant Rock. A cool breeze tickled the sweat pooling on my forehead. We climbed at a steady pace, and the path wove in and out of the shade. Small wooden bridges crossed stream beds. Birds sang, and my children chattered, grateful to have their dad on the adventure.

Three-and-a-half miles from the trailhead, we arrived at the lookout point near Elephant Rock.

Martin eyed the gigantic boulder tucked in a crevice down a few yards from the trail. "Come on. Let's climb it," he said and led the way.

I scrambled after him, slipping and sliding down the short, steep dirt path to the rock. At the base of the white granite pillar, I stopped. Fifty feet above me, Martin balanced on a ledge and beckoned me to follow.

I tried. A few feet in the air, I got stuck. The white wall, inches from my face, obscured my view. I stretched to grasp a handhold. Nothing.

Martin called down. "Move your right hand up and to the right. Great. Now move your left foot to that small crevice. Push up and grab with your left hand." He coached me the entire way.

The climb was short as far as rock climbing goes. Though not technical or very difficult, it challenged me. My stomach tightened and tumbled. My arms and legs quivered. I followed his instructions with precision. Ten minutes later, I joined my husband on top.

Glorious and triumphant, we surveyed the scene below. The foothills folded into each other from north and south. They stretched on until they gave way to miles of buildings and roads. In the far distance, we saw the Great Salt Lake glittering in the afternoon sun with Antelope Island jutting into the skyline. William took our picture and captured the trees, city, and lake as a backdrop.

I had trusted Martin as my guide. He had experience with climbing and had scaled several man-made walls in the past. He knew what he was doing and had the added benefit of seeing what I couldn't see from his vantage point on top. I let go of my plans and followed someone with a better view and more knowledge. The reward was breathtaking.

It's the same with our interactions with God. Because He "knoweth all things, and there is not anything save he knows it" (2 Nephi 9:20), we can trust Him. We can let go of the control and let Him orchestrate our lives. Just like Martin didn't tell me the whole route up the rock all at once, the Spirit guides us a little at a time, bit by bit, as we're ready for it. This was the pattern God follows in life, and the one He followed during the donor assessments.

Each day we inched closer to Glenn's final testing. At length the transplant team cleared him to take the cross match and tissue typing tests. These were the final, expensive tests they would allow only one person to take at a time. Tissue typing compared genetic markers from both parties to see how many matched. There had to be enough for a successful transplant. The cross-match was like a mini transplant test. It took a vial of Glenn's blood and mixed it with Martin's. Once they combined the two blood samples, they could look and see if Martin's body contained antibodies that would reject the foreign organ. If not, then they'd be good to go.

These tests were so complex that it took two to three weeks to obtain any results. With eager anticipation, we waited.

As we waited, unforeseen glitches arose.

Glenn's results showed some aberrations that might or might not be serious. He discussed them with his primary care doctor, but without more information, they wouldn't know for sure. It would be best if Glenn got more answers before he committed to donating a kidney.

We prayed Glenn's health would be fine as uncertainty wracked Martin's family. First, Rolf had been diagnosed with liver cancer and died from it. Then, Martin had been diagnosed with kidney failure.

Now, Glenn faced an unknown diagnosis that might prove devastating. All within twelve months.

With faith in God and a deep love for his brother, Glenn assured us he was still willing to donate after they got the complications cleared up. But he wouldn't know the answers for a while. If we wanted to wait a few months to find out about his health, he was still willing. If we wanted to proceed with me, he would totally understand.

The love of Martin's brother humbled us. Glenn kept fighting for a way to donate, despite all the roadblocks. But waiting for answers meant waiting that much longer for Martin to recover, waiting that much longer with him barely existing.

Hope died. Tension, anxiety, and fear soared. Fear for Glenn. Fear for Martin. Fear for me. On my knees, I cried in anguish to Heavenly Father. We had come this far. Why? Why couldn't these complications have arisen three months earlier? Why get our hopes up only to have them dashed? What were we going to do now? It kind of felt like the Lord had backed us into a corner and left us with no choice but for me to proceed.

Me? Really? The girl who had fainted at the sight of blood? I managed to get through the testing, but surgery? Sure, I'd improved with the blood thing, yet I was still the girl with an ultra-low pain tolerance, the girl who couldn't make it through the birth of my first child without a second epidural. How would I do this? I didn't fear death. That was too remote. The pain of recovery? That frightened me.

Martin, on the other hand, faced bleak nightmares and feared the worst would happen. With all that he had been through, he shrank in horror at the decision we faced. Nevertheless, we had to decide.

We consulted with our transplant coordinator, and Vicki took the information to the decision-making body. Considering Glenn's new data, the transplant team consented to let me proceed with the tissue typing and cross-match tests. We decided to do that.

Just because I proceeded didn't eliminate Glenn. Who knew? Maybe they'd clear up his health questions in a week or two. My testing merely gave us more information with which we could make a choice. For all we knew, my organ would not be a suitable match.

My test results came back a few days before Thanksgiving.

Compatible.

The time had arrived. The final decision had to be made. But before we could make that decision, we needed one more piece of information.

"We have a question," I said to Vicki over the phone. The morning was quiet with all the kids gone to school. My transplant notebook lay open on the kitchen table. Notes and details covered several pages. Pen poised, I was ready to jot down more notes. We had to get this right. We needed all the information we could get before approaching the Lord.

"Sure. How can I help?" Vicki's confident, compassionate voice reassured me.

"Well, I know you can't tell me about Glenn's cross-match test because of privacy and everything." With my voice was full of anguish, I pushed on. "But is he a better match for Martin? Would it be best to wait? Because he's a sibling?"

"Michelle, it's just a number. And you're not a number," she said, her voice soft and caring. "The most important indicator of a successful transplant is not the quality of a match."

"It's not? But . . ."

"Matching is important. That's true, but it only goes so far. The biggest factor in how long transplanted kidneys last is how careful the recipients are to take their meds on schedule, every day, at the same time."

"At a specific time? I didn't realize that?"

"Yes. Twelve hours apart. Every day. For the rest of the kidney's life. That's the most important indicator of long-term success. If you and Martin decide for you to be his donor, you can rest assured your kidney is a suitable match. Otherwise, we wouldn't consider you."

I hung up the phone and dropped my head into my hands. Deep down, I had been feeling that I would be the donor. I'd resisted the impressions until that time. Now we had more than just feelings. We had information. Now we could "study it out" (D&C 9:8) in our minds, make a choice, and ask God to confirm our decision.

In his first general conference address as prophet, President Russell M. Nelson talked about employing this process in choosing his counselors. He said, "Because I know that good inspiration is based upon good information, I prayerfully met one-on-one with each Apostle"

("Revelation for the Church," 94). Armed with knowledge, he took his decision to the Lord to choose his counselors.

The time had come for the Lord to reveal His will, for us to know His thoughts. Armed with knowledge, we decided and prayed about it. The Lord confirmed our choice. I contacted our coordinator and committed to move forward as Martin's donor.

CHAPTER 13

WOULD THAT I MIGHT NOT SHRINK

"[I] would that I might not drink the bitter cup . . . Nevertheless, glory be to the Father, and I partook and finished my preparations."

(D&C 19:18–19)

"Are you okay?" the kind visitor asked when she saw my agitation and the tears pooling in my eyes. It was four days before my wedding, and I was at a neighbor's house for a mid-week Relief Society activity to learn how to make homemade rolls. Most of the women there were my friends and understood the drastic changes coming to my life in less than a week. One of them hugged me as I stumbled through an explanation to this person who didn't know my history. How did I say that getting married petrified me? Would she understand why I didn't want to back out?

Yes, getting married terrified me. Not the getting married part. I loved my fiancé with all my heart. He was the man I waited many years to find, and I was excited to spend eternity with him.

The dread and anxiety came because I would become an instant mother to four children. How could I do that? What if it didn't work out? Neighbors and strangers alike had bombarded Martin with horror stories about blended families. What if they were right? What if the kids never grew to love me? What if I never bonded with them?

It didn't matter how hard it would be. None of my fears altered my course. I had committed not only to Martin, but to William, Adam, Katie, and Brian. The Spirit of the Lord had confirmed my decision. Trusting in Him, I would move forward.

Each of us faces things we've committed to that fill us with anxiety, dread, or fear, even if the result might be good: giving birth, starting a new job, moving. We move forward with trembling trepidation because we know it's the right thing to do. The month of December before my surgery was like that.

I fretted and stewed over the pain that loomed large in my future. I worried about all the little details. What would happen during recovery? Both Martin and I would suffer at home, in the same bed, at the same time. Who would take care of him? That had always been my job. I couldn't do it. I'd be too sick to do it. Who would take care of me?

Who would take care of my children while I was in the hospital and when I got home? How would it all work out? The kids needed love and strength and guidance. They needed their parents, yet both parents were going into surgery.

While I waded through those heavy doubts, immense relief flooded my entire body. At last! We had a plan. No more spinning wheels, just waiting. This is the stage I'd prayed for months would come. It didn't matter that Glenn wouldn't be the donor. It was time to move forward. I loved my husband and my children. God loved us. We had a good life.

Through all the stress and anguish, we needed to remember that. How could I remind my family of all we had, especially at Christmas, the season we remember Jesus Christ more than at any other time?

I looked at the pictures from 2011, the awful year of dialysis, the year of stress and worry. The photos revealed a more complete story. They were evidence of a good life.

Nicole grinned and held her award at sixth grade graduation. Dennis, perched on the high dive, waved at the camera. Brian balanced on his older brother's back at his Eagle court of honor. Katie posed with her roommates. Martin and I witnessed an encroaching cloudburst in the mountains during our June hike and enjoyed the fall colors of our October hike. The pictures continued. They showed love, happiness, family.

This is what we needed to focus on at Christmas, not health and hospitals. I forsook decorating the tree with the usual ornaments. Instead, I printed several pictures of every family member, all taken in 2011. I hole-punched them, laced yarn through the holes, and hung them on the tree. All of them took delight in finding themselves on the tree that season.

But even the Christmas tree seemed to sense the drama unfolding and reacted accordingly. Martin and I had put up a live Christmas tree most of our married life. The tree of 2011 is the only tree that fell apart, literally. Each time someone looked at a picture, bumped it, or jumped in the front room, hundreds of needles tumbled to the floor. By Christmas, most of the branches hung bare except for the pictures and yarn, showing both the good and the bad.

Stress and anguish. Gratitude, love, and determination. My emotions rode a fast roller coaster. Up and down. Faith and peace followed by doubt and terror. Too often, the dread won. Worries became more and more irrational with each passing day.

One evening after the sun had set, the early winter darkness seemed even darker than usual as I left the Costco parking lot. I pulled my van to the exit, paused at the stop sign, and checked for oncoming traffic. Bright headlights zipped by, one after another. The glaring lights dazed me. My fingers clenched the steering wheel. Were all forty-thousand people who live in Bountiful, Utah, out on the streets Christmas shopping that night? They drove so fast. What was the big hurry?

A small break came. I held my breath and stomped on the gas pedal. The large Honda Odyssey engine took hold and thrust me into the traffic. Safe. But to my worried heart, I was only a fraction away from the onslaught of oncoming headlights.

What if I'd been in an accident? What if I got in an accident before the transplant? What if I died before I could give Martin my kidney? What then? My driver's license indicated that I'm a registered organ donor. What if the emergency doctors whisked away my kidneys and gave them to random strangers? What would happen to Martin?

With quivering hands and a pounding heart, I completed my trip. I gave my husband a shaky hug as soon as I got home.

Martin, too, suffered from fears and worries. The demons that haunted his dreams were the same nightmares he'd faced since August. Over and over, he posed the same questions to himself, to me, and aloud when no one was in the room to listen. How could he ask me, his wife, the mother of his children, to make this immense sacrifice? It was his job to protect his family. Subjecting me to major surgery was not protecting them or me.

Irrational terrors asserted themselves. Little voices proclaimed the worst-case scenarios. His questions spiraled downward, running rampant in his mind. The doctors said they've never had anyone die during surgery, let alone both the donor and recipient. But they also said there is no guarantee. What were we doing?

Logic told both of us these fears were irrational. If they'd been actual threats, we never would have proceeded in this direction. Even so, worry and anxiety battled calm and peace for supremacy.

I knew it was possible for God to remove the burden from my shoulders. He could heal Martin. Over the past six months, I had pled numerous times with Heavenly Father to fix it, to make it go away. He didn't.

Jesus Christ also faced the darkest period of all history with trepidation. Though we don't know His specific thoughts, we do know He cried out in anguish, "Abba, Father, *all* things are possible unto thee; take away this cup from me" (Mark 14:36, italics added). Three of the four New Testament Gospels record a variation of the same phrase (see Matthew 26:39, 42, 44 and Luke 22:42). Latter-day revelation expounds on it. Christ described the atonement this way, "Which suffering caused myself, even God, the greatest of all, to tremble because of pain, and to bleed at every pore, and to suffer both body and spirit—and would that I might not drink the bitter cup, and shrink" (D&C 19:18).

Though I loved my husband and was eager to donate my organ to save him, the transplant was more challenging than anything I'd ever done before. When we are faced with trials more arduous than we imagined, we can draw strength from knowing that God, Himself, also conquered the darkest moments of His life. His victory makes it possible for Him to help us do all we need to do during our dark, desolate days. As Elder Neal A. Maxwell said, "Jesus pressed forward sublimely. He did not shrink, such as by going only 60 percent of the distance toward the full atonement. Instead, He 'finished [His] preparations; for all mankind" ("Swallowed Up in the Will of the Father," 24).

I had prayed many times for God to make it all go away. As I prayed and struggled, I came to accept His will. Martin and I did not shrink; we continued.

The first week of December my intense final screening began as I met with various members of the transplant team. It felt like déjà vu; I met the same group of people at Martin's intake interviews. I thought I knew what to expect. Blood tests, counseling, release forms, and so on.

A surprising but important interview took place with the social worker. Martin held my hand during this meeting, as he'd done during all the others. He gave me strength and comfort.

"We need to ask you to leave, now," she said to Martin.

We exchanged puzzled glances. What did she want?

"We need to ask Michelle some private questions."

"Okay." Martin squeezed my hand before he stood and walked to the door. The door shut behind him and left me alone with her.

"Are you donating your kidney of your own free will and choice without coercion?"

"Yes." I spoke and nodded at the same time to emphasize my answer.

"What if Martin doesn't take care of the kidney and he loses it? How will that impact you?"

I paused and bit my lip while I composed my answer. This was a heavy question. I wanted to get it right. I didn't want them to disqualify me. Besides, I trusted Martin and knew he would take care of this precious gift. But, what if . . .? That was the question they wanted me to answer.

A huge breath escaped, filled the silence, and then I answered, timid but honest. "I would be disappointed. I can't deny that. But this is a gift. What he does with this gift is his choice. I hope he would do all in his power to preserve the life of the organ, and I believe he will.

But if not, it doesn't change the fact that I want to donate my kidney to save his life. I love him."

She nodded her encouragement, took notes, and proceeded. "Is there any reason at all that you would not want to do this?

Tears filled my eyes as I stared into hers. With every fervent emotion I could muster, I said, "I want to donate my kidney to my husband. I consider it a sacred honor, and I want to do it." I did not want them to mistake my choice in this matter.

The social worker smiled and jotted notes down on her evaluation paper. "I thought as much," she said. "I could tell before I asked, but I still needed to ask. I can see how much you love each other. Your husband can come back in and finish your appointments with you now."

Upon reflection, I could see how this conversation and my answers mirrored the Savior. Regardless of Martin's future decisions, I loved him so much that I wanted to offer this gift to him. Regardless of our actions and decisions, the Savior loves us so much that He willingly gave his life for every single individual who ever lived on the earth, even those who reject Him in the end.

After that important interview, my testing continued. They repeated many of the blood tests I'd already received. One showed a blip that concerned them. My kidney function was worse than last time.

"Oh," I said with a half-chagrined chuckle. "I donated blood a few weeks ago. Would that make a difference?"

It did. Strike that problem from the worry list. They cautioned me not to donate blood again before the surgery. I promised I wouldn't. And I didn't, even when the ARUP called me at home because a little one at Primary Children's Medical Center needed blood. As soon as I told the lady on the phone what I was doing, she wished me well and reassured me I was doing enough in the donation field. They would find someone else. Still, my sadness at not being able to donate showed how far I had come since my first attempts.

I also had to get a CT scan of my abdominal section. The images would show the doctors my kidneys so they could evaluate them before they gave their final approval.

The technician took me back, settled me on the table, and sterilized my arm for the needle they would use to insert the contrast. I glanced at it. Bad choice. It was huge. Larger than any needle I'd had inserted into my veins before.

She brought the monstrous object to my arm and poked. I tried not to wince. She shifted and jiggled the needle. The pain rose. I held my breath. She tried again. Nothing.

Abandoning that arm, she tried the left one. I held my body still and squeezed the rubber ball she'd placed in my fist. She wiggled the needle, pulled it out a fraction, shifted angles, and thrust it deep into my arm again. Every muscle and nerve tensed tighter than before. She twisted it around again before she gave up and sought help.

I fought back the tears and tried to breathe slowly and deeply. In. Out. In. Out.

The supervisor arrived. Back to my right arm. With a sharp jab and a few twists, she inserted the needle correctly.

I exhaled a big breath and sank onto the bench. The torment had passed. All I had to do was wait until the scans were done.

"Okay, now we're going to send the contrast in. Your arm will burn, but it shouldn't be that bad."

Not that bad? Then why was she warning me?

"Three, two, one."

Ten seconds later the burn seized my entire arm and upper body. Now I knew. I tried not to think about the blazing heat, but how do you not think about your arm on fire?

The burning stopped, and the whir of the machine silenced. I let out a deep, shaky breath. I'd survived that, but how would I survive the operation?

Nestled between the CT scan and another appointment were parent-teacher conferences. Usually, we didn't have much to discuss with the teachers. This time was different. Brian, who was a senior, couldn't afford to have any mishaps. Nicole was in her first year of junior high and needed all the support she could get. Dennis, who was in the third grade, needed an understanding teacher as well. Every teacher needed to know about the upcoming transplant and be prepared for how it might impact our children.

I had to leave Nicole and Martin before we finished at the junior high for an appointment with a psychologist. His job was to evaluate my mental stability and capability of dealing with a transplant. Like all the other meetings, he, too, had the ability to reject me as a donor. Knowing how terrified I was of the surgery, I approached this interview with taut nerves, hoping he would not veto my donation because of my fears.

I sat in a comfortable leather chair in his office. A soft glow filled the room as the sun dropped toward the horizon. Rows of bookshelves lined the walls. An atmosphere of calm peace permeated the room and helped me relax.

His kindness and empathy lowered the remaining barriers. We discussed my thoughts, feelings, and fears. He told me it would be unusual if I wasn't afraid. Not to worry. As we talked, the Spirit filled the room. Feeling safe, I declared I knew God had guided this process and led me to this point. At the end of our two hours together, I had renewed strength and peace.

During this same time, Glenn received devastating news. The health situation he'd experienced appeared to be worse than anyone had suspected. He had a ninety-five percent chance of a serious medical problem. An exploratory procedure was scheduled.

We prayed for Glenn while he underwent the procedure. To our great relief, surprise, and gratitude to God, he received good news. The procedure revealed an anomaly. Glenn was in the five percent. He did not have the serious problems the earlier tests had indicated. He was fine.

The incredible news came after I had completed most of my screenings. This was no coincidence. God had removed Glenn from the donation list until it was too late. Then, in His mercy, God made it known that nothing was wrong. In awe and humility, Martin and I realized, once again, we knew God's will. He wanted me to sacrifice my kidney for my husband.

In an email update to family and friends, I wrote: "As we have watched since last April, I can see the Lord's hand guiding this process. Indeed, many roadblocks were encountered by those who volunteered. On the other hand, every test and every step of the way for me has been quick, easy, and unfettered. I truly believe this is the Lord's will."

I still had one appointment left. The surgeon had the final say, and God's will continued to be revealed. She approved my surgery.

While I sat with her, I asked a question that had troubled me. "This may sound silly," I said, somewhat embarrassed.

"It's okay. What?" Her kind voice encouraged me to proceed.

"What if I'm in an accident and die before surgery? Can Martin still get my kidney?"

She smiled and reassured me it was not an unusual question. Many prospective donors have similar irrational fears. She guaranteed I could designate Martin as a recipient, in case something happened. She explained further that they didn't whisk organs away at the scene of an accident. The next of kin had to give permission regardless of what the driver's license said.

The final meeting passed, and everyone involved approved of my organ. The months of testing and preparing were completed. We had done everything we could think of to be ready. We mirrored the Savior in preparing and moving forward despite anguish and fear.

Christ finished everything He needed to do to complete His final mission in life—the atonement. Each of us has a different calling in life. Sometimes we don't want to do what God asks. When we move forward with faith to finish the work He gives us, He will open doors for great miracles. President Howard W. Hunter said, "All of us must finish our 'preparations unto the children of men.' Christ's preparations were quite different from our own, but we all have preparations to make . . . [which] often will require some pain, some unexpected changes in life's path, and some submitting" ("The Opening and Closing of Doors," 59).

We had pain. We had unexpected changes. We had to submit. As we did all those things, we found ourselves ready not only for the surgery but for great spiritual outpourings from God, before and after our operations.

CHAPTER 14

GOD SENDS ANGELS TO OUR AID

"And there appeared an angel unto him from heaven, strengthening him."

(Luke 22:43)

The sun shone through the windows, making the room in the Salt Lake Temple even brighter as light bounced off the mirrors hanging on opposite walls. It was 2007, four and a half years before transplant, and Adam would leave on his mission in less than a month. William had returned from his mission six weeks earlier. Martin and I wanted to do sealings with them while they were home together. The sealer had reserved my favorite sealing room, the one connected to the celestial room by a flight of stairs.

Martin escorted me to the altar in the bride's place, then took his spot across from me. A huge smile grew from my mouth to my cheeks and eyes. I'd spent hours researching my ancestor, Millie Smith, and now she was being sealed to her second husband, Wells Tyler. Brilliant joy saturated my body as her emotions penetrated the veil and infused my soul. It was one of the strongest witnesses I've had in the temple of the reality of those living beyond the veil. Angels are real.

As transplant neared, my witness of angels grew. Many of the angels who came to my aid were family and friends. As Elder Jeffrey R. Holland said, "not all angels are from the other side of the veil. Some of them we walk with and talk with—here, now, every day" ("The Ministry of Angels," 30). My personal army of angels came from everywhere, giving me both physical and spiritual assistance.

Martin and I had hoped we could have the operations during Christmas break. But in the middle of December, our coordinator, Vicki, informed us that wouldn't work. Two of the three surgeons were going to be gone after Christmas. They scheduled our transplant for Monday, January 9, 2012.

At first, I was disappointed. It would have been nice to have my children home from college to help take care of the house, the kids, and Martin and me during recovery. On the flip side, now we could enjoy Christmas at a slower pace.

As soon as Christmas passed, I flew into a flurry of activity. There were so many things my grown children wouldn't be available to do because of the timing shift. The to-do list seemed never-ending. Discard the poor Christmas tree without needles. Put away the holiday decorations. Make some freezer meals for the family. Arrange rides for Nicole and Dennis to get to school. Compile a list of emergency contacts. Confirm that my niece, Sally, would stay with the kids during our days in the hospital. One by one, I checked off the tasks.

We'd be in recovery for two to three weeks after we got home. How would we make it all work? Ramen noodles or mac and cheese would keep the kids alive. Not the most nutritious, but they wouldn't starve. More pressing was the question of how we were going to get Martin to and from the hospital for his triweekly labs.

Visiting teachers came to the rescue. A sunny afternoon the week before surgery, they entered my house armed with a notebook, paper, and instructions from the Relief Society president.

"How can the ward help, Michelle?" Kathleen asked.

"Oh, thank you so much. The reality is, with both of us down, we will need help."

Kathleen jotted down notes while I listed off the tasks, meals, and rides. She added house cleaning to the list. After the business was done, the three of us chatted. We laughed. We cried. We shared spiritual stories. I bore witness to them of Heavenly Father's involvement in this process. In turn, they testified to me about His love and concern for us.

Kathleen reached across the couch and took my hand. "The Spirit's so strong. It's almost tangible."

"It is." I nodded. "It is." I gave them each a hug before they left. Their angelic visit had transformed my living room into a sacred haven that lifted my soul and blessed it.

The minutes stretched on, and the days zipped by.

A family friend called and asked if he could come and visit on Saturday, two days before the operations. Gabriel had donated a kidney for his father three years earlier. We were eager to talk with him, to learn more about what to expect from someone who'd been through it before. He could tell us the bald truth.

Gabriel walked into our living room carrying a laptop. The house was clean and calm. The kids were at a movie, giving us time to learn from Gabriel. Martin and I sat on the couch next to each other. He took a seat on the recliner perpendicular to the couch. A few minutes later, he shifted the chair so he could look us in the eyes without hindrance.

"So, how are you two doing?" he asked. He comprehended our emotional, spiritual, and physical state more than anyone else we'd talked to recently.

We sighed, held hands, and looked at him.

"I think we're ready." Martin said.

"I just want to get it done," I said.

"I understand. That's why I wanted to come today," he said. "To share my experience and answer any questions you might have."

He shared his knowledge and gave us several tips he'd learned from his surgery. Stitches at the surgery site would be painful, but they'd be secure and wouldn't tear. We should take a back scratcher and lip balm to the hospital. If we hugged a pillow against our stomachs when we sneezed or coughed, it would ease the pain at the incision sites. It was important to walk every day, even if we didn't feel like it, because walking sped up recovery. We needed to be patient during recovery because it might take months longer than the doctors indicated to regain our strength.

He paused and opened his laptop. "Let me show you some pictures." He turned the screen so we could see it. "Here we are in the hospital. And this is the day we were released."

Gabriel shared some of his and his family's sacred experiences and the beautiful miracles they witnessed. He testified of Jesus Christ and His atonement and the sacred nature of transplant. A reverent tone replaced the light, casual atmosphere in our room.

Tears ran down my cheeks as I listened. I leaned closer to my husband and rested my head against his shoulder.

"Donating my kidney was one of the best things in my life. One of the hardest, but one of the best. I would donate another if I had three. Your love for your husband will grow. Your love for the Savior will grow."

I nodded. It already had.

"You will be sustained by God's love. He will be with you the whole way. Don't worry about how hard it will be. That will pass, and then you'll have this beauty the rest of your life."

After two hours, Gabriel stood to leave. I noticed the room had taken on the soft glow that comes with twilight. The lighting matched the quiet mood and emphasized his testimony.

"Thank you," Martin said. "You came to us today with more than facts and horror stories, which is what we thought we wanted. You reminded us of the sacred, spiritual nature of this event."

"Yes," I said. "You set the stage perfectly. Thank you."

He departed, but the Spirit he brought remained. His visit was the perfect beginning to the following week.

Sunday began bright and early. I had one last errand I needed to accomplish before I could surrender to the doctors. My temple recommend needed to be renewed because it would expire at the end of January.

Before I went to the stake office, I called to ensure I could meet with someone who didn't have a cold. The last thing I wanted was to get sick and have to recover from an illness at the same time I recovered from surgery. Or worse yet, get a cold and then give it to an immune-suppressed Martin. The clerk assured me everyone was well.

"So, you've got surgery tomorrow?" the stake presidency member asked as I entered his office. The stake clerk must have spread the word.

"Yes, it's the kidney transplant," I told him.

"Oh?" he asked, "so it's you, not your husband?"

"No. It's both of us. I'm his donor."

He stopped. After a few seconds, he looked at me and said, "That is a very sacred thing."

He proceeded to ask me the standard questions. As it does each time I answer them, my faith in Heavenly Father, Jesus Christ and the gospel grew stronger. I left surrounded by a cocoon of love and peace regarding the upcoming operations, grateful for President Olson's ministering as a representative of the Lord. The recommend questions reminded me God was in charge. He watched over His Church and His apostles; He watched over my family and me.

In the evening, several family members came to our house to end a family fast and pray together. Our sons dragged chairs into the front room to accommodate our six children and daughter-in-law, Martin's parents, my parents, my siblings and sister-in-law. Many extended family members joined through an Internet video conference. Their love traveled through the digital air waves and embedded in my heart.

After the prayer, we disconnected the video call and prepared for priesthood blessings. My brother, Neil, anointed my head with consecrated oil. My father gave me a priesthood blessing of protection, healing, and comfort. Martin, his father, and our sons joined the circle. The righteous men of God repeated the same process for Martin.

The Spirit of God filled the room. Unseen angels—family members who had departed—joined their faith with ours and succored us.

All week long, angels had ministered to us: my visiting teachers, the stake presidency member, Gabriel, and others. They hovered near, strengthened, lifted, and prepared me. These angels were God's messengers of love, mercy, and hope. Now spiritual angels joined their efforts with the others.

As Elder Holland said, "From the beginning down through the dispensations, God has used angels as His emissaries in conveying love and concern for His children. . . . most often [their purpose] is to comfort, to provide some form of merciful attention, guidance in difficult times" ("The Ministry of Angels," 29).

The help of ministering angels is a beautiful mirror of our Savior's life. During his darkest hour, "there appeared an angel unto him from heaven, strengthening him" (Luke 22:43). Before Gethsemane, other angels had visited Him, too. At the end of his forty-day fast—after He had battled Satan for the third time—"angels came and ministered unto him" (Matthew 4:11).

The Lord always sends help when we need it. He said, "I will go before your face. I will be on your right hand and on your left, and my Spirit shall be in your hearts, and my angels round about you, to bear you up" (D&C 84:88). God sent mortal angels to bear us up. He also sent spiritual angels to our aid.

I remember one occasion several months before Martin's diagnosis. We had been living with the problems his illness caused, even though we didn't know what was going on. Since he couldn't work and our finances had plummeted, depression and discouragement often threatened to overtake me. Prayer brought relief. Most of the time, it came through peace delivered by the Holy Ghost. One time, though, He sent an angel who understood my trials.

Sleep had evaded me that discouraging night as thoughts of mounting bills and our struggles kept me wide awake. While I lay there, I sensed the presence of two ancestors from beyond the veil. I knew them. I'd done temple work for both. One was Millie Smith, the woman whose joy had consumed me at her sealing.

She'd been raised in Palmyra, New York, in the mid-1800s, after the Saints had left. She and her husband died in Michigan. Why had they moved? A land record explained part of the story. Economic disaster. They'd sold their Palmyra home in foreclosure. Millie knew hard financial times. She understood my turmoil.

I opened my heart and listened.

She had a distinct message for me. "Hang in there. It's worth it."

Her love, along with the love of the other heavenly visitor, soothed my aching heart. I gained courage to "hang in there." Months later, we discovered Martin's health problems and took steps toward recovery. She was right. It was worth it.

Angels are real. They had ministered to my children in the past, and I knew they would during the tough days of transplant.

After Martin and I received our priesthood blessings, I asked for our children's attention. They were scattered on the couch, pillows on the floor, or wooden kitchen chairs. I shifted my gaze from one to another until I'd looked at each of them.

"The Lord will be with you this week," I said. "He will send angels to watch over you while we're gone. Mamma Sherri will be with you. I can't be here to take care of you, but she will. All six of you. Even you, Nicole and you, Dennis."

The Spirit bore witness to me that I spoke truth. Just as I loved and cared for Sherri's birth children, she did the same for mine. I didn't realize at the time just how predictive my words would prove to be.

At the time of transplant, Dennis was nine years old and in the third grade. I can't imagine how terrifying it must have been for an innocent child to be old enough to understand his mom and dad were going to the hospital, but not old enough to make sense of the details. He absorbed the stress and anxiety that invaded everyone, but he didn't know how to talk through it. Would he be okay while I was gone?

A few days after I came home from the hospital, Dennis went on a walk with me.

"Tell me what you did while I was in the hospital," I said.

"We got pizza one day." My sister, Kim, had stayed with Nicole and Dennis on the first day. She had distracted them with pizza and a movie.

"Yum. I didn't get any. What else?"

"I got a ride to school every day."

"Oh, so you went to the Cook's house in the morning?"

"Yup, and Sister Cook took me to school."

"That's nice. Anything else? How did you *feel* while we were in the hospital?" I said.

"Mommy Sherri came and comforted me once when you were gone."

"Oh, what happened?"

"Brian and Sally made me go to bed while they watched TV. I was mad because I didn't think it was fair, since Brian has to get up earlier than I do."

I could picture the entire scene. The TV was giving them badly needed dead-brain-cell time. Dennis wanted to join; he hated going to bed anyway. But his brother and cousin sent him to bed despite any tantrum he might have thrown. I could imagine him arguing and eventually stomping to his room, with no one realizing he was scared, anxious, and didn't want to be alone.

Dennis continued. "That's when she came."

"How do you know it was Mamma Sherri?"

"Because I said a prayer and asked for her to come. Then I felt this burst of warmth. That's how I know."

Miracles haven't ceased. "Nay; neither have angels ceased to minister unto the children of men" (Moroni 7:29). Elder Holland said, "God never leaves us alone, never leaves us unaided in the challenges that we face. . . . we may feel we are distanced from God, shut out from heaven, lost, alone in dark and dreary places. Often enough that distress can be of our own making, but even then the Father of us all is watching and assisting. And always there are those angels who come and go all around us, seen and unseen, known and unknown, mortal and immortal" ("The Ministry of Angels," 31).

The love and peace from both Heavenly Father and His divine messengers carried and sustained me the next day during the surgery and the coming days ahead.

CHAPTER 15

A FOCUS ON JOY HELPS US ENDURE

*"Jesus . . . who for the joy that was
set before him endured the cross."*

(Hebrews 12:2)

The taillights of Mom's car grew smaller and smaller. Tears streamed down my cheeks as I waved goodbye.

She had brought me to Rexburg, Idaho, to attend Ricks College, with more than enough stuff for any freshman. Knots had held my stomach captive all day while we'd unpacked, made my bed, decorated my room, and stowed my dishes in the kitchen cabinets. Her enthusiasm at my new apartment did little to assuage the trepidation that tightened every nerve of my body.

All throughout my entire senior year in high school, I'd looked forward to the day I could go to college. Now the day had arrived, and I didn't want her to leave me. That shouldn't have been a surprise. Though independent, sometimes to a fault, I still leaned on the strength and support of home. I was the only one of my five siblings to cry on the first day of kindergarten when my mom left. Why shouldn't I cry now? Being alone, five hours away from safety and security, panicked me.

"Can I stay home in December and not come back to Ricks for the second semester if I want to?" I asked before she left.

"Yes, you can. But you won't want to. You'll love it."

She was right. I loved college life, living away from home, and being an adult. The future joy was worth every bit of the anguish at the initial departure from home. Faith in her words at the joy that would come gave me courage to do the hardest thing I'd ever done in my life to that point.

The same anticipation of a brilliant future gave me courage to face transplant surgery, another one of the hardest things of my life.

A sharp trill of my alarm awoke me in the wee hours of the morning, long before the sun rose on January 9, 2012. I hadn't slept well. Nerves kept me awake. Nerves and the bowel prep I had to take Sunday night. No problem. I had plenty of time in the hospital to catch up on my sleep. Oddly enough, I arose in good spirits. Finally. At last. It was time.

Both Martin and I had to fast before the surgery, so getting ready didn't include breakfast. After a quick shower, I put on sweats and rejected makeup. I couldn't stand my breath, and brushing my teeth never seemed to do enough when I was fasting. A half-stick of mint gum should help.

The time had arrived to go. My small overnight bag contained toiletries, a back scratcher, and my own pillow. Anxious and eager to be gone, but not prepared to leave, I let out a deep breath and glanced around the front room. Was everything done? Even the previous night found me putting the final touches on the day-to-day schedule for the kids. How would they manage with their dad and me in the hospital? I wouldn't be here to get them off to school or greet them when they came home, to answer questions about surgery, to hug them when they got scared.

At least I could hug them now. I could comfort them now.

Leaving my bag by the front door, I moved to Nicole's room. I opened her door, crossed to her bed, and nudged her awake. "Honey, we're leaving," I said.

The sleepy thirteen-year-old sat up and put her arms around me. I squeezed her and held on for a time. The embrace grew tighter with each passing second.

"I love you, sweetie." Tears threatened, and I gulped them back.

"I love you, too, Mom. Aunt Kim promised she'd take Dennis and me to the hospital. We'll see you soon."

"William's going to call the school throughout the day with updates." I pulled her close and stroked her hair. "And remember, if it gets too tough to stay in school today, you can leave. I gave you a note. The neighbors said they'd come and get you and take you home if you need to. Just call them. It's okay if you do."

Martin came in and gave her long hug too. "I love you, Nicole." He kissed the top of her head and rested his cheek on her hair for a moment.

The two of us moved to Dennis's room.

I sat on his bed and tugged at my deep sleeper. He stirred, and I pulled him into my arms. "Dad and I are leaving now."

"Bye, Momma. I love you."

Dennis climbed out of bed, and Martin drew our young son into his arms.

"Bye, Daddy. I love you."

"I love you, too. I'll miss you, but we'll be home before long." Was he saying this to reassure Dennis or himself? Probably both.

"Remember," I said, "when Nicole leaves in the morning, go next door to Sister Cook's. Aunt Kim's going to be here after school today, so you won't have to be alone."

Thank goodness I had my sister. She loved my children, and I knew she'd care for them well on that first day, the worst day. One last hug, and I turned to leave. The little boy settled back down in the dark room.

William was already in the car, warming it up. Brian, who was up and getting ready for school, walked to the car with us. We gave him a big hug and told him we loved him. We'd given our hugs to Adam and Katie the previous night, before they headed back to Utah State University. Our children had been through so much already, and today would be difficult for everyone. The last words had to be about love.

William pulled away, and Brian stood in the driveway, waving. We waved back until he disappeared from view.

The sun still lingered behind the Wasatch Mountain range when we drove into the parking lot. My parents and Martin's parents were already there when we arrived along with Martin's older sister, Jolene. She couldn't donate, but she could be there with us, loving and sustaining both of us before the surgeries and supporting her parents during them. We checked in, and they ushered me to one surgical prep room and Martin to a different one. My mom and dad came with me, and Martin's family went with him. William bounced between the two rooms, carrying news back and forth.

I changed my clothes, donned a blue hospital gown, and climbed onto the hard hospital bed. Bright red toenails with a white flower on my big toes poked out where the blanket quit covering my legs. No hospital socks for me. The surgical staff needed something pretty to look at while I was out. Many of the nurses commented on them, which made me smile, and I needed all the smiles I could get.

The pre-op nurse grabbed a clipboard and started asking the pre-surgery questions. "When did you eat last?" The flat tone of her voice hinted at the number of times she'd asked these questions in the past.

"Last night about 7:30."

"Good." She made a note on her chart. "How about the bowel prep? Any problems?"

"None."

"Good," she said again. Before the next question, she glanced up and froze.

"Are you chewing gum?" Her voice sharpened.

The half stick of mint gum felt as large as the entire package. "Yes," I said hesitantly. Confusion reigned, along with the faintest hint something wasn't right. At the age of forty-five, no one had chided me for chewing gum in years.

"But you said you hadn't eaten anything since last night." Her voice grew more urgent with each word.

"I haven't," I said.

"Gum counts. This is bad. They might not do the surgery." She rushed off to double check. Like a chastened school girl, I spit out my gum, chewed my lip instead, and tried to hold it together.

The nerves in my stomach multiplied as I considered what this might mean. They might have to postpone the surgery. If they did that, who knew when they'd reschedule us? This isn't something you can just schedule any day of the week.

Besides, being on the docket didn't guarantee the transplant would happen as planned. They could have bumped us off the schedule with only a few hours' notice. If a deceased donor's organ became available, they'd transplant it first because those organs had a very short life-span before they were rendered useless.

We hadn't been bumped. We were finally here at the hospital. Now this? "Please don't let them halt everything over a little piece of gum," I prayed.

Another CNA scrubbed my arm, inserted the drip-line needle, and finished prepping me, just in case they would proceed. They wanted me ready the minute the operating room became available. My parents sat in the two empty chairs in the room. A few minutes later, my husband joined us along with everyone else. Together we awaited the news, conversation subdued.

The nursing staff came in and out handling the many tiny details necessary before a surgery. Half an hour later, I ventured to ask one of the staff, "Are we still having the surgery?"

"Oh. Yeah. They said it would be okay since it was only gum. But don't chew anymore." My shoulders relaxed, and a smile eased my taut facial muscles. I laughed. "Definitely." The uncertain tension in the room subsided. Comfortable laughter at light-hearted jokes filled the space and quieted my nerves.

Martin came to my side for a picture, both of us wearing hospital gowns. His gown didn't cover his long torso as well as mine covered me. At least he had hospital pajamas to provide some modesty.

The nurse walked in with a blue disposable hair covering. "It's time, Mrs. Christensen." She handed the cap to me, and I tucked my shoulder-length hair into it. The light banter my family shared ceased, replaced by nervous smiles. Months of medical testing, stressing, and praying had come and gone. The first of the long-anticipated operations had arrived.

"I'm ready." I looked at the large analog clock on the wall. Eight forty-five. "Just a few more hours until it's over." I took a deep breath. I just wanted to get on with it.

Martin leaned down, gave me a kiss, and squeezed my ice-cold hand; I clung to his hand. He had the largest hands of any person I knew. These were the hands that had rocked my fussy babies to sleep when no one else could and stroked my hair to ease my tension during stressful days and nights. These were the hands that rested on my head during priesthood blessings. These were the hands of the man I loved most in the world.

His left ring finger looked bare without his wedding ring. Both of us had complied with surgical instructions, and his ring nested atop my wedding bands, safely tucked in our dresser. I rubbed his empty finger and couldn't wait until we could both wear the symbol of our eternal love again.

My eyes locked onto his deep-set blue eyes. I smiled. "This is good. God has led us here. This kidney will give you a new life."

He wrapped his arms around me, careful not to disturb the protruding IV needle. "I love you, Michelle," he said in a hoarse whisper against my ear. "Thank you."

We held hands as our family approached with hugs and wishes of good luck. I got a hug from my son, who carried the burden of communicating the news, good or bad, with his siblings. My sister-in-law, the one who had bravely tried to be the one in my spot, hugged me next. Martin's parents approached and embraced me, their eyes reflecting love and gratitude for the sacrifice I was making to save their son.

Last, my parents wrapped their arms around me. I couldn't imagine the emotions they experienced as they were about to watch their daughter be wheeled away. Odds were in my favor that all would go well, but I was positive the "what-ifs" lingered in their minds. Yet, they loved my husband too. Since my sacrifice could help him, they supported our decision.

The heartache and longing they felt mirrored that of our Father in Heaven when "he spared not his own Son, but delivered him up for us all" (Romans 8:32). President Dallin H. Oaks said, "Think how it must have grieved our Heavenly Father to send His Son to endure incomprehensible suffering for our sins. That is the greatest evidence of His love for each of us!" ("Love and Law," 26).

In that moment, I understood my Heavenly Father better. Just as my parents were there, loving and supporting me, Heavenly Father is there for us. Always. He loves us with a love we cannot understand. President Thomas S. Monson assured us, "God's love is there for you whether or not you feel you deserve love. It is simply always there" ("We Never Walk Alone," 124).

The nurse retrieved the fluid bag off the rack and secured it to the bed. An orderly lowered the head and dropped me into a reclining position. He unlocked the wheels and pushed me out the door. Another attendant joined him and helped move the unwieldy gurney.

I looked at my mom and dad. I looked at Martin's parents, my sister-in-law, our son. I looked at my husband. I tucked all their love and prayers into my heart.

My eyes stayed locked on Martin's as long as they could, while I traveled down a long hallway that ended way too soon. His eyes watched and prayed—hurt, humility, and gratitude showing in them. I smiled and waved goodbye before we turned a corner.

The orderlies pushed the contraption down one corridor after another. I stared at the passing dots on the ceiling tiles.

Peace through the atonement of Jesus Christ had banished the intense fear I'd lived with for months. It arrived Saturday when Gabriel had visited. It cloaked me on Sunday at my meetings and pierced my soul during the evening's priesthood blessings. Peace walked out the front door with me when I left home that morning. Now it rode with me to the surgical floor.

I knew it would be okay. Still, nerves danced up and down my stomach. Questions lurked underneath the surface.

How well would Martin's surgery go? Would his body accept the kidney? Would he get better? The medical team had cautioned us that transplant was only a treatment, not a cure. I couldn't wrap my head around that. Not yet. Martin had been sick for so many years.

I prayed my sacrifice would make the difference in his life. That he would no longer have to exist on dialysis, only to die in a few years. A new kidney could let him live many more years, let him help his children navigate the difficulties of growing up, marrying, and raising their own families. It could allow him to serve in the Church and build God's kingdom.

He had to get better. I *needed* him to get better. I wanted my husband cured.

I prayed for Martin, and I prayed for myself. Peace covered the doubts that tried to surface and kept them subdued. God had led us this far. I needed to remember that. I inhaled a deep breath, let it out slowly, and steeled my mind to focus on God's promises of the future.

The orderlies maneuvered the gurney around a corner and followed a winding path into the elevator for the three-day, thousand-mile excursion to the surgical floor. When the elevator stopped with a tiny jolt, my stomach lurched a hundred feet. The doors slid open, and they wheeled me down more winding passageways until we entered a long, sterile corridor.

Barren walls with no pictures stretched down as far as I could see from my reclining position. Random carts full of supplies peppered the hallway. The orderlies halted my bed by a closed, steel door and left. The sign next to the door read, "Transplant and General Surgery."

A few minutes later, a nurse came to my bedside. "The OR isn't quite ready yet. You'll need to wait here."

"Okay," I said, not trusting my voice to speak more than that.

"In a few minutes, the anesthesiologist will come and talk to you."

I turned my head on the pillow to look at her.

"Then we'll take you in when the room's ready." She left.

I stared at the dots in the tiles overhead and waited. Metal doors down the hallway thudded. Wheels squeaked on carts and beds that were rolled up and down the corridor. People clothed in green scrubs came and went.

The anesthesiologist came and leaned over me to make eye contact. He explained the medications he'd give me. I bobbed my head up and down like I comprehended all the medical terminology he spouted. I didn't. He assured me he'd be present the entire time, monitoring my vitals. That's all I needed to understand. He left a few minutes later.

I waited.

The nurse joined me again. "They're almost ready." She took my glasses and stowed them in a bag attached to the end of my bed. "They'll be there when you wake up. Any last questions?"

Questions? Of course. But she couldn't predict the future. I shook my head, and she disappeared again.

I waited. Alone.

The moment had arrived. The most frightening thing I had ever done in my life was here. It would be worth it if Martin could regain his health. I loved him so much, and that love sustained me and helped me face my fears of pain, surgery, and recovery. I would give anything for him. It would most definitely be worth it.

Even if Martin's body rejected my kidney that day, it would still be worth it. If the kidney failed soon or waited for ten, fifteen, or twenty years to fail, it didn't matter. All that mattered is that he had the opportunity to live. This was the best chance I could give him.

I wonder if similar thoughts went through the Savior's head in Gethsemane and on the cross. Did He think about how much He loves us, about *why* He was making the sacrifice? We don't know. What we do know is that His strength to overcome came from joy. The Apostle Paul said, "for the joy that was set before him [Jesus] endured the cross" (Hebrews 12:2).

I never understood that scripture until President Russell M. Nelson explained that joy brought power to the Savior. "Think of that! In order for Him to endure the most excruciating experience ever endured on earth, our Savior focused on joy! . . . Surely it included the joy of cleansing, healing, and strengthening us; the joy of paying for the sins of all who would repent; the joy of making it possible for you and me to return home—clean and worthy—to live with our Heavenly Parents and families" ("Joy and Spiritual Survival," 83).

None of what the Savior suffered mattered to Him. He loves us so much. That is how he carried our burdens without resentment. All He wants is for us to return home to Heavenly Father and be like Him. His perfect love even reaches out to those who reject His gift. He wants them to have the chance. The future is all that mattered to Jesus Christ, and it gave Him strength.

Lying there in the hospital, the future was all that mattered to me. It gave me courage and strength to face one of my biggest trials. None of my struggles mattered: not the finances, not the lonely days, not my fears of physical pain. None of it mattered. The only thing that mattered was that my dear husband had a chance for a new life.

With joy, I faced the future.

The nurse returned. "We're ready now." She smiled and pushed my bed into the operating room.

"It's really cold in here," I said, wondering how I was going to endure such a frigid room for several hours during the operation. The nurse agreed and turned her attention to the IV.

When I surfaced several hours later, every tiny movement seared my abdomen with bolts of excruciating pain.

CHAPTER 16

The Power of Prayer and Priesthood Blessings

Jesus "blessed them, and prayed
unto the Father for them."

(3 Nephi 17:21)

The first time I remember the power of God in my life, I was seven years old. A deep, wracking cough had awakened me. Chills and shivers ran up and down my arms. My eyes burned and my forehead was on fire. In need of comfort, I climbed out of bed in search of my mom and found her and Dad relaxing in the front room, watching TV.

"Mom," I said, "I don't feel good."

She pulled me in and kissed the side of my forehead. My fever must have been soaring because Dad made a phone call and left the house.

He returned with a man from our ward, our home teacher. Brother Jones anointed my head with consecrated oil. Then Dad and this kind man laid their hands on my head while my father gave me a priesthood blessing.

When it ended, Brother Jones shook my hand. "You'll be better in the morning."

Next morning, my cough had disappeared, and my fever had vanished. Mom kept me home from school just in case I got sick again. I didn't understand why. Brother Jones promised me I'd be better, and I was.

Heavenly Father hears our all our prayers: the prayers given by worthy priesthood holders, the formal prayers we give when we kneel alone or with others, and the silent, heartfelt prayers we utter throughout the day. Martin and I received the benefit of all three types of prayers before, during, and after our surgeries.

Our son, William, who was at the hospital with us, recorded the events of transplant day in an email to friends and family who prayed on our behalf. Following are several excerpts from his email along with details I learned from my family later.

WILLIAM

We got to the hospital at around seven a.m. and checked in to the prep rooms. Mom went in first with her parents to a prep room down the hall, and Dad went in shortly thereafter.

We waited for a few minutes and then met with Dad's surgeon. He was very kind and seemed extremely knowledgeable. He asked about Dad's current health and showed us where the kidney would be placed. Dad spoke with him about the current meds he was taking and asked a few other questions.

Shortly thereafter, I went searching for my mom's room. I found it, and she was a little worried because she had been chewing gum. Kind of funny that something as small as gum had caused so much worry. The nurse informed her that this might delay the surgery. Right after I got there, the nurse came back and informed us that as long as Mom stopped chewing the gum, she was okay to go ahead.

Mom and Dad shared one last embrace, gave each other a big kiss, and Mom went off to the OR around eight forty-five a.m. Grandma and Grandpa Dennis (GnGD) came with [me], Grandma and Grandpa Christensen (GnGC), and Aunt Jolene to Dad's room where we talked about what an amazing, sacred sacrifice Mom was making for Dad. The spirit was very nice there.

After a short time, Grandma Dennis decided it was probably a good idea to go upstairs and wait in the surgery waiting room in case they needed to find her. Dad agreed, and GnGD went upstairs to wait. This was about nine-thirty a.m.

We didn't wait too much longer, and we were on our way, following Dad up to surgery. They took him to the beginning of a long hallway and wheeled him out of view.

Then began the long wait. . . .

GnGC, GnGD, Jolene, and I tried to find something to distract us for several hours as we waited in the surgery waiting room. Every so often we would hear news that Mom was in surgery and doing well or that the kidney was on the move. They delayed Mom's surgery a little bit because of the rooms getting a little mixed up in the OR, but in the end they got her situated and got everything underway. Dad waited outside the hall for about forty-five minutes for his turn before they took him in and got started.

At around eleven-thirty they took Dad into the OR, and we waited.

Around one p.m. or so, Mom's surgeon came out. She explained that Mom's surgery had gone well! She was all stitched up, and the kidney was on the back table getting worked on so it could be put into Dad. Dad was opened up and ready to receive the kidney, and they were ready to get going.

The surgeon explained that Mom would be in recovery for another hour and a half and then be in her room. Shortly thereafter I was off. . . . Down the hall and out the front door to Costco. Earlier that morning, Dad had given me money and instructions to make sure Mom had a dozen roses waiting for her when she got in. With the roses in place, we were ready for Mom's arrival.

During the long day, my family told us they prayed for the health of Martin and me. As they prayed for others, God strengthened their hearts and gave them renewed peace, faith, and courage.

Prayer gives us power to continue on our journey. President Henry B. Eyring said, "As the forces around us increase in intensity, whatever spiritual strength was once sufficient will not be enough" ("Always," 9).

So many times in my life, prayer has replenished me during an ongoing struggle or difficulty, and I have wished the peace and strength from a single prayer would last longer than it does. However, as President Eyring warned us, opposition around us intensifies. As mortals, we don't have the strength to move forward without continuous divine help. That help comes from constant prayer. When we pray, it opens a portal for God to meet us at our current level, in our current circumstance, whatever it might be.

My family members and others prayed for us. I'm certain their prayers helped the doctors. I'm also certain that through their acts of faith in praying for us, God lifted their own burdens and gave them greater ability to cope with the uncertainty of waiting.

Praying for others is a mirror of Jesus, who always prayed for others. Just like the prayers we offer for others impact us, the prayers our perfect, resurrected Savior offered for others impacted Him. In 3 Nephi 17, we read about the beautiful blessings and prayers Jesus offered on behalf of the Nephites. After he finished praying for the children, verse 22 records, "And when he had done this he wept again."

Prayer strengthens and lifts us. Prayer can heal us, especially prayer offered through the power of a priesthood blessing. God does not answer all prayers and blessings the way we want: with healing, health, and happiness, like my experience as a young girl. In both the cases of Martin's first wife, Sherri, and his brother-in-law, Rolf, they received priesthood blessings, but the Lord gave a different answer than all their family desired. But there are times when God grants healing blessings with a direct, immediate miracle, which is how He blessed Martin during his problematic recovery from surgery.

Down in the recovery room, I had a hard time coming out of the anesthesia. As I surfaced, sharp, jabbing bolts of pain shot through my abdomen. Even the tiniest of movements bombarded my senses with agony. I needed help. Where was help? The medication still held my body hostage, and I couldn't say anything to get the aid I sought. Maybe if I raised my hand, they'd notice I was trying to get their attention and needed help. Nothing. Just more pain. Did they give me more medication? I don't know.

The drugs pulled me under again for a time. I drifted in and out of consciousness. Each agonizing, wakeful period lasted longer than the previous one. Eventually, it was time to be wheeled out of recovery and to the tenth floor.

The orderlies pushed my bed into my room. My parents were there and gave me a soft hug. Red roses from Martin sat on the nightstand. On the white board hanging on the wall by my bed I saw the words, "Sarang Hae," a Korean phrase that is an expression of love reserved for the deep love between husband and wife. Martin must have enlisted help from William, and Martin's love and thoughtfulness warmed my heart a few minutes before the medication claimed my conscious thought.

The minutes crept by. An attached pain pump became my best friend. One push and my body could succumb to the relief of a drug-induced sleep that stilled my body and held back the lightning bolts of pain. I drifted in and out, hugged the pillow I brought from home to my chest, and held motionless as much as possible because each tiny movement ignited the fire and seized my abdomen.

At some point, Martin's parents and William came to my room. I don't quite remember when. Martin's surgery must have finished. It was after four. That seemed like a long time. But . . . sleep overtook me again.

Two more hours passed. Still no Martin. My parents went to eat, and when they returned, Don, Arda Jean, and William left to get some dinner. Mom and Dad settled down again into the slightly comfortable chairs in my room. Dad pushed the recliner out and let his feet come up.

"Mr. Christensen? Mrs. Christensen?" A voice came over the speaker in the room.

I stirred. *What?*

"Hello. This is Michelle's mother."

Oh, good. Mom's here. She'll take care of it.

"No. I'm sorry. Wrong Mrs. Christensen."

"Can we help you?" my mother asked, concern in her voice.

"No. I need to talk to a family member of Martin Christensen. Do you know how I can get in touch with them?"

"They're at dinner."

"Okay. I've got a cell phone number for Mr. Christensen's contact person. I'll call him." She disconnected and left a heavy silence in the room.

"That doesn't sound good," Dad said at last.

"No, it doesn't," Mom agreed.

The seconds stretched on.

Dad's right, that doesn't sound good. Oh well. They'll take care of it. My foggy brain didn't register the seriousness of the situation.

William recorded this in his email: "While we were at dinner, I got a phone call. The PA wanted to see us in the surgery waiting room. She said Dad was having a tough time waking up, and they were not sure what was going on. [She] explained she wanted to be sure he was safe, so they were considering putting him in the ICU overnight to make sure he woke up all right. We asked if we could administer to him, and she said she would check and give me a call when they knew more."

William and Martin's parents returned to my room.

A half hour lapsed, Martin did not come. Permission for a priesthood blessing did not come. News of his recovery did not come. Nothing came. Another half hour passed, and then another.

Don stood. "Martin needs a blessing." He strode out of the room.

"Martin. Martin!"

"Why wouldn't they just leave me alone," Martin said later when he retold his experience. "I just wanted to sleep, but they kept waking me up."

They called his name, "Martin."

He groaned. "What . . ."

"Breathe!"

Oh. That's what they wanted. Martin took a deep breath. A minute later, blackness took over again.

"Martin. Breathe."

He took another breath.

"If you can't wake up, you'll have to go ICU." The doctor's firm voice reached through the darkness.

Martin forced another breath. He faded again. Then he felt heavy hands rest on his head and heard his father's familiar voice.

"Martin Don Christensen, in the name of Jesus Christ, I command you to wake up."

William explained what happened this way: "Grandpa Christensen, Grandpa Dennis, and I placed our hands on Dad's head and gave him a blessing. During the middle of his blessing, Dad's respiratory rate dropped to a seven. It should be at around seventeen. Then as soon as we took our hands off his head, it raced upward to a twenty and then rested around sixteen to seventeen."

After the blessing, Martin recalled that the doctor stepped forward, put her face right in front of his and said in a serious and firm tone. "You have to stay awake, or we'll put you in ICU. You've been here too long. If you can stay awake, I'll send you up to the floor. It's your choice. Can you stay awake?"

He assured her he could.

"We left Dad there in the recovery room," William wrote, "and waited another hour or so is all, and they told us the good news that Dad was on his way up to see us all and be on the floor with Mom."

Before Martin would be content going to his room, he insisted on seeing me. The orderlies wheeled his bed down the hall and stopped it in front of my open doorway.

"Hi, Michelle," Martin said and waved at me.

I looked to the door, and with my head still collapsed on the pillow, raised my hand a fraction and waved back. The orderlies reversed their direction and pushed Martin to his hospital room, three doors down. Later, he talked about how hard it was for him to see me in that condition, barely able to lift my head. His gratitude for my safety, his appreciation for my sacrifice, and his guilt at causing my pain all filled his heart with deeper love for me.

We were both alive and on the road to recovery.

The power of the priesthood, the power of God Himself, penetrated the heavens that day. Following the example of Jesus Christ, worthy men authorized with God's power laid their hands on Martin's head. They blessed him to recover. President Russell M. Nelson said, "When you lay hands upon the head of another, you are not offering a prayer, which of course requires no authority. You are authorized to set apart, to ordain, to bless, and to speak in the name of the Lord" ("Personal Priesthood Responsibility," 46).

They spoke in God's name, and He answered.

That day He answered our cry for help with an immediate yes. In His wisdom, our Heavenly Father doesn't always give us an immediate, miraculous healing. To help us become who He wants us to be, His answers may be neither quick nor easy, as we were about to find out during our long recovery.

CHAPTER 17

ENDURING TO THE END

"I . . . finished the will of . . . the Father."

(D&C 19:2)

The mountain wind whipped my face in June of 2004, eight years before transplant. Martin and I stood on the summit of Mount Timpanogos, 11,752 feet in the air. We reveled in our triumph and the breathtaking view that stretched below us. Utah County and Utah Lake spread to the west. On the east, layers of Wasatch Mountains unfolded until they gave way to the Heber Valley. The fatigue, pain, and discouragement of moments before vanished. We had climbed over four thousand feet from base camp, a feat I'd wanted to do for years but never dared attempt.

I'd accomplished the goal, but the hike wasn't over. The descent included over seven-and-a-half grueling miles. Footstep followed footstep on the downward path that wound on and on and on. Blisters, dehydration, and fatigue walked with me every step of the way. Would it ever end? All my training had not prepared me for the excruciating, exhausting downhill trek and the mental stamina that had to accompany the never-ending journey.

Fourteen hours after we left in the morning, several hours after most hikers had returned, Martin and I straggled into the parking lot. Relief washed over my weary body. It was over. With victory complete, now I really had something to celebrate.

Transplant was just like that hike. Surgery was the summit. I had reached the goal. Life was good. Then the painstaking road to recovery began.

After they wheeled Martin to his room, most family members left. Martin's sister, Jolene, volunteered to spend the night to help if needed. All I needed was to sleep, which I did.

Martin did not. He lay wide awake. The pain escalated with every passing minute. The doctors refused to give him any opioids because of how long it took him to wake up in recovery. To make things worse, he received a massive dose of prednisone to suppress his immune system. Agitation skyrocketed.

Jolene was asleep in my room. At two in the morning, she jolted awake. *"Martin needs me."* Thirty seconds later, she poked her head into his room.

"Martin, you're awake," she said, surprised. "How are you doing?"

"Not good," Martin said. He described what was going on.

Jolene pulled a chair close to his bed. How could she distract him? She asked about his children. Martin talked. When they exhausted the subject of family, she asked about the latest in space exploration, a topic that fascinated Martin. He talked some more. Question after question, the night wore on. Jolene kept the demons away until sunlight and hope arrived with the new day.

Of course, I had been oblivious to those long, dark hours and learned about them later. All I knew were the nighttime interruptions of blood draws, medication dosages, IV drip changes, and, of course, pain. Pain disturbed my sleep the most. Each time I shifted, blazing bolts shot through my abdomen.

In the morning, the nursing staff brought me a fresh cup of ice chips. The cold relieved my parched mouth and left me satisfied. Food was not appetizing.

"Hi, Michelle," said a tired, familiar voice that reached my ears from the hallway.

Mustering every ounce of energy I possessed, I shifted my head toward the sound. Martin stood hunched in the doorway and gripped an IV pole. He shuffled into my room and reached for my hand. A nurse was beside him, one hand placed on his back to steady him if needed.

I couldn't believe it. A delighted smile filled my face. We chatted all of thirty seconds until his wobbly legs inspired the nurse to usher him back to his room.

I dropped my head back onto the pillow and groaned. As much as I loathed the idea, I had to get up. Not yet. . . . Later. . . . Much later. With a pillow clutched to my stomach, I slept.

A nurse came into my room later in the morning. "It's time to walk." Her voice was chipper and full of confidence. "The faster you get walking, the faster you'll recover."

She undid the leg massagers, raised the head of my bed, and pushed my blanket away. "Stay on your side while you drop your legs over the edge."

Agony soared. "It . . . it hurts." My voice was sharp and high-pitched. "My stitches. They feel like they're tearing out."

"You're okay." Her words were soft and kind. "I promise; your stitches are secure."

I followed her directions.

"Now, grab hold of the bed railing and push yourself to a sitting position. Just like that."

Heavy breaths escaped from my mouth with each tiny movement.

"Rest for a minute and catch your breath," she said. "You're doing great."

I sat with my feet dangling, each intake of air full of torment. A moment later, I resumed.

"Ease your feet onto the ground. Yes. Good. Keep going. Here's the IV pole. Hang onto it. I'll walk beside you and make sure you don't fall."

With clenched teeth, tight shoulders, and heavy feet, I pushed one foot forward and took half a step. I held my breath and shifted the other foot forward. Five excruciating minutes later, I poked my head into Martin's room. "Hi, Martin," I said. "I beat you up this time."

"Hey, look at you. You're amazing."

"Isn't she doing great? The nurse praised me along with my husband.

"I'm going back to bed now." I turned and started the marathon-excursion to my room.

My kind helper supported me as I sat, eased my way down to rest on my side, and shifted me onto my back. My heart swelled with gratitude. I couldn't believe how much love I felt for a stranger, a person I might never see again after her shift ended in the evening. My CNA was the same, always full of hope that filled my soul and helped abate the mental torture of pain.

Three hours later, the nurse helped me walk to Martin's room again. He was up, and we walked around the tenth-floor loop together. A few hours later, we walked three laps without the aid of the nurses. They cheered us on each time we shuffled past the nurse's station, like we were winning the Boston Marathon.

The nursing staff rotated in and out; I rarely saw the same person more than once, yet I trusted each one. All the nursing staff had received special training in transplant care, and all knew how to help mitigate the pain. They encouraged me when I walked the halls and were attentive to my needs. Their watchful care comforted and lifted me.

During the week, family and friends dropped by, sent flowers, and prayed for us. Each of our kids called or visited. My sister Kim had planned on bringing Nicole and Dennis to the hospital on the first day. But given the difficulties of recovery, she shielded my youngest two from the trauma. Instead, she treated them to McDonald's and a trip to the dollar store where they could buy anything they wanted up to ten dollars each. They were in heaven. On the second day she brought them to see us, took them home, and returned to stay overnight in my room. William stayed overnight in his dad's room.

The outpouring of love in the hospital surprised me. I had expected grueling, unrelenting agony to reign supreme. Instead, everyone from the nursing staff to friends and family brought love that nurtured, lifted, and healed me. Each wove their way into my heart. They loved me and I loved them back. As Joseph Smith said, "it is a time-honored adage that love begets love" (Smith, 517).

Best of all, Martin's new kidney worked. He felt more normal than he had in years. His brain fog left, the metallic taste disappeared, and the bone-weary fatigue departed. Wednesday, two days after the surgery, he started a liquid diet of Jell-O and soup. On Thursday, they transitioned him to regular food—as regular as hospital food can be, that is.

He was the one who met with the pharmacist, the nutritionist, and the doctors. He was the one who concentrated and learned what medications he needed to take every day, the signs of kidney rejection, and how long he had to stay isolated after he got home. He was the one who took notes and managed all the details I'd handled the past nine months, the details he couldn't sort out earlier.

I didn't fare so well.

The surgeon had shifted around all my insides because she had to move the organ from the back of my body to the front where the incision was. My insides rebelled and shut down. The doctor changed my pain medication, hoping to wake up my sluggish stomach and bowels. It didn't work.

On Thursday, my diet still consisted of ice chips only. They told Martin if he wanted, they'd let him go home. He didn't want to leave without me and stayed. By Friday, the doctors said he was ready. I was not.

"I feel guilty going home without you." Martin said to me. "I hate to leave you here alone. Do you want me to arrange for your sister to stay overnight with you?"

"No, I'll just sleep. Really, I'm fine." Staying one more night sounded good to me. It gave me twelve more hours of security before I had to recover on my own.

Saturday, the doctors could hear gurgling in my stomach. They felt confident discharging me from the hospital. I wasn't so sure. I still couldn't eat anything. Every sip of grape juice sat on my stomach and didn't move.

Emotionally, I wasn't ready to go home either. Normal responsibilities faced me even though I had no strength to do them. Plus, how would I recover at home without trained medical help? Who would assist when I needed to get out of bed? Bring me food when I was too weak to move? Encourage me when the pain and weariness threatened to control my mind? Martin couldn't take care of me. He had his own recovery.

Ready or not, the hospital staff released me on Saturday. The downward trek began.

Adam drove to the hospital with Martin, who endured the painful, jolting drive so he could be with me. His love and gratitude for me shown in his eyes the minute he walked through the door. Before he left home, he wrote this on his social media page:

"Michelle Dennis Christensen saved my life with a living kidney organ donation Monday, January 9th. I can never repay this gift of life. I am awed by her courage and generosity of spirit. We spent the last week together in the hospital, walking the halls. She has suffered great pain and illness. But with the faith and prayers of many friends and family she has steadily improved. She will come home today to a hero's welcome.

"Our greatest thanks to the doctors, nurses, and other professionals at Intermountain Transplant Center. Their passionate compassion is evident in the excellent care we are receiving. Second to none!

"Michelle, I Love You."

I was so glad to see him, so grateful he was doing well. My eyes locked with his, and my love for him soared to greater heights.

Martin wore his new, forest-green T-shirt that read "Recycle Life," a gift from the transplant team. I wore my matching navy-blue T-shirt, and we got several side-by-side pictures before we left.

The nurses wheeled me outside, and Adam opened the van door. I eased in and clutched my pillow to my stomach for the jarring ride. He pulled away from the sanctuary that had been my home for six days.

Thirty minutes later, Adam eased the van into the driveway. One shaky foot after another, I climbed the four steps leading to my front door. After a few triumphant pictures, I walked inside, ready to lie down. At a snail's pace, I made a beeline for my bedroom.

Once we returned home, the love and care we felt in the hospital continued. Adam and his wife stayed with us through the long Human Rights Day weekend. They and the kids fixed us breakfast, brought us pain meds, and filled our hearts with joy. My system awoke, and I could digest food again. It was progress.

Early Monday morning, Adam drove Martin to the hospital. A blizzard raged. Snow piled on roads the plows had already passed over.

It blanketed both the town streets and the freeway. The treacherous drive was necessary. We were so grateful that Adam had come home to help.

Martin needed his transplant meds checked at the hospital lab at precisely six in the morning on the dot. The medical team who monitored his blood work needed instant access to his numbers. Later in the day, the nurse called and gave Martin instructions to adjust his meds.

All too soon, the long weekend ended. It was time for my college-aged children to head back to Logan, Utah. I waved goodbye to the taillights that drove our twenty-four-hour care away. Loneliness filled my soul as I shuffled back into the house.

The next several days passed in a blur of pain. Nausea flared if I let my pain killers wear off. It came when I didn't take the meds with food. It slept with me after I ate. I was miserable.

Though miserable, I determined to continue the pattern I set in the hospital and walked as much as I could. Sometimes Martin and I made our way outside when the ice and snow didn't pose the risk of slipping and falling. At other times, I shuffled down the short twenty-foot hallway in my home, made a gradual arc to turn around at the end, and retraced my steps.

I remember one specific hallway trip. I reached the end of the hall and started the turn. Pain, tears, nausea. All of them flared.

"If I had known it would be this difficult, I don't know that I would have done it."

I still have a vivid memory of thinking those exact words.

Regardless of how I felt, I couldn't just stay there. Just like on my trek down the mountain, I had to get back. I had to finish. I gathered my courage, took another step, and finished the length of the hallway. I turned around and did it again and again.

The Savior is an excellent mirror we can look to about finishing. Though He suffered in Gethsemane, His course was far from complete. He endured mock trials during the night, scourging in the morning, and crucifixion in the afternoon. In His misery, He comforted others. After death, He established missionary work in the spirit world. After three days, He was resurrected. He had to do all of these things before He could say, "I . . . accomplished and finished the will of . . . the Father" (D&C 19:2). Even now, though the atonement is complete, He still has work to do; He is still helping us, comforting us, acting as our advocate so that we can return to Heavenly Father.

I realize the Savior had a choice, and He *chose* to finish. On the other hand, surgery eliminated my choice. Once they removed the kidney, I had to recover. However, that fact did not eliminate my choices; it changed them. I had to choose how I would recover. I could have stayed in bed and let the operation set me back further than necessary. Instead, I gathered my courage, faced the rocky trail down the mountain, and finished my trek.

All of us have a journey to complete, even when it isn't easy. At times you might feel like I did and think: "If I'd only known, I wouldn't have done it." During these difficult times, Elder Dieter F. Uchtdorf encouraged us to keep moving forward. "Even when you fail, you can choose not to give up, but rather discover your courage, press forward, and rise up. That is the great test of the journey" ("Your Great Adventure," 87).

The test of our journey intensified after our college-aged children returned to school. We couldn't drive, but Martin had to go to the hospital three days a week at six in the morning. We couldn't bend, twist, or exert ourselves to clean the house. We couldn't lift over ten pounds.

The good news was we didn't have to trek down the mountain by ourselves. Our ward family helped us on the long path of recovery.

One day, the first week we were home, the doorbell rang mid-morning as I sat in the front room. Two women stood on the threshold, with cleaning supplies and friendly smiles. One made her way to the bathroom, and the other started in the kitchen. I returned to the recliner. The sweeping rhythm of a broom and the sounds of a brush scraping the porcelain toilet bowl filled the house. When they left, the house glistened and smelled fresh. Two more came the following week and two more the week after.

Three days a week, the alarm rang a little after five. Martin pushed himself to his side and dropped his feet to the ground. He struggled into sweatpants and a T-shirt. Another day of labs. Ward members picked him up and drove him thirty minutes to Murray, Utah. They waited while the labs were drawn, sometimes more than a half hour.

Then, they drove him back home. They did this for three weeks, all before sunrise during January's short days.

Evening arrived and brought another knock on the door. Two more sisters from the ward greeted us, holding dinner. They crossed the floor to the kitchen and deposited homemade soup, hot rolls, a green salad, and brownies. "We hope you're getting better. Good bye." They disappeared as fast as they arrived.

Martin called our children together for dinner. He prayed before we ate. "We thank, Thee, for the love and charity of our ward family. We pray for them."

The food was manna from heaven. "How can we repay all the kindness?" I asked Martin.

"We can't. We can only pay it forward."

Without help, we couldn't have done it. Elder L. Tom Perry discussed how the ability to endure is better when we are "an integral part of the community of Saints . . . each of us has a role to play, each of us is important, but in order to succeed we must be unified in our Savior" ("The Gospel of Jesus Christ," 46).

Sometimes we are the receivers and sometimes the givers. Either way, when we are unified, the Lord can bless us. Joseph Smith said, "if one member suffer all feel it—by union of feeling we obtain pow'r with God" (*Joseph Smith Papers*, 61). We suffered, and they helped us. After we healed, we helped others who suffered and helped them heal. Service, love, and actions like these join us together. The more unified we are, the closer we approach exaltation. No wonder Jesus prayed "That they all may be one; as thou, Father art in me, and I in thee" (John 17:21).

As great as the power was that we received from others' help, it wasn't enough for Martin. Grit and determination weren't enough. A problem arose that required extra help.

Because Martin's new kidney was working, the doctors could remove the dialysis catheter with confidence that Martin wouldn't need it anymore. After the simple, routine procedure, the surgeon approached me.

"The surgery went well," he said.

I smiled. So far, everything was working out. Martin felt better than he had in years. His kidney function soared. Now, the last tie to dialysis had disappeared. We had turned a corner on the path to better days.

"But I have some concerns. His incision is not healing right."

The words stopped me cold. Not again. Why did Martin always seem to be part of the one percent with strange complications?

"The bottom half is weeping fluid," he said. "I opened it up while he was on the operating table today. Now it will heal from the inside out. I stuffed gauze into the open wound to absorb the fluid. Bit by bit, the opening will heal and close."

That didn't sound too bad. Longer than expected, but doable. My shoulders relaxed until I heard the doctor's next words.

"He needs the gauze and bandages changed twice a day. Either here at the clinic or at home. It's your choice."

I stared at the kind man. I knew what that meant. Because of the incision's location, Martin couldn't change it himself. It fell to me. Really? Despite transplant, I still hated medical procedures. Besides, what about my own recovery?

But it had to be done. Better for me to do it at home than spend an hour driving to and from the clinic twice a day. I'd done difficult things before. Surely, I could do this.

The assistant showed me what to do. Each morning and night, I changed the gauze in the open wound. As predicted, the incision healed bit by bit.

Martin had done all he could do, but it hadn't been enough. He had to rely on me to complete his journey, to finish healing. So it is in life. We have to rely on the Savior's grace. The Bible Dictionary says, Grace "is divine means of help or strength, given through the bounteous mercy and love of Jesus Christ. . . . [it] is an enabling power that allows men and women to lay hold on eternal life and exaltation."

Without the grace of God, it is impossible to descend the mountain path whole and well. Nephi said, "after ye have gotten into this strait and narrow path, I would ask if all is done? Behold, I say unto you, Nay; for ye have not come thus far save it were by the word of Christ with unshaken faith in him, *relying wholly upon the merits of him who is mighty to save*" (2 Nephi 31:19, italics added).

We need the Savior. We need others. We need courage. As Elder L. Tom Perry put it, "Enduring to the end is definitely not a do-it-yourself project" ("The Gospel of Jesus Christ," 46).

With the help of all three, we reached the end of our journey. April 9, 2012, arrived. Transplant quarantine ended, and Martin could go out in public again. We had trekked up and down the transplant mountain. We went to a restaurant and a play to celebrate.

But that's the thing about mountains. There is always another one to climb. All too soon, God sent another hard mountain for us to scramble up.

CHAPTER 18

SURRENDERING TO GOD'S WILL

"And ye shall offer for a sacrifice unto me
a broken heart and a contrite spirit."

(3 Nephi 9:20)

After transplant I had smiled and relaxed, secure in the notion that the Lord had given me the biggest trial of my life, and I'd passed. Now I could rejoice in the knowledge I'd been tested and found sufficient. I was ready to proceed with a comfortable, easy life of building God's kingdom.

It didn't take long for me to realize just how wrong I was.

As time went on after transplant, I understood more and more the concept that transplant was a treatment and not a cure. The medical staff's reluctance to rush into transplant made sense. It would have been far better if Martin's kidneys could have rebounded, because he never regained his full strength and health.

The immunosuppressant drugs gave Martin awful side effects, which linger through to this day. Yet, he has to take them twice a day, every day. Thirty minutes after swallowing the pills, his cheeks, chin, forehead, and scalp grow numb. His hands and fingers burn. His feet tingle and hurt. Acid reflux rises in his chest and burns his throat.

Sixty minutes after the first tingle, the effects fade bit by bit. Two hours after the dose, he's back to normal—on good days.

On bad days, the medications trigger a migraine. He can't take the same pain relievers he took before transplant. Aspirin and ibuprofen harm kidneys. Tylenol provides minimal relief.

Even so, we are grateful because Martin is so much better than when he was on dialysis. Remembering the torture of those treatments helps us keep his current health situation in perspective. At the time he suffered through dialysis, I thought it was a waste of precious time that kept us from moving forward, from moving toward the goal of transplant.

Instead, it turned out to help not only Martin's immediate health, but it helped the future too. As bad as some days after transplant were, we knew it could be so very much worse. President Dieter F. Uchtdorf's words proved true in our case. He said, "Often the deep valleys of our present will be understood only by looking back on them from the mountains of our future experience" ("Continue in Patience," 58).

Over weeks, months, and years, Martin adjusted to less-than stellar health. He learned to live with the side effects of the anti-rejection meds. He had more good days than bad.

Our finances recovered, and we paid our debts. Martin celebrated with our children as they grew, graduated, and served missions. He lived to see the oldest three marry and meet new grandchildren. He took our family to Palmyra and Nauvoo. Our life was good.

Then my world tumbled around me again. God asked for a new, devastating sacrifice.

Five and half years after transplant, Martin had an annual exam with his urologist. Routine blood work showed Martin's prostate-specific antigen (PSA) count—the measurement that often predicts cancer—was too high. Normal is below four. The troubling number from 2011, the number that sent us to visit Dr. Kinder, was just above six. In 2017, the number registered more than nine.

A biopsy confirmed our worst fears. Prostate cancer.

Martin was only fifty-seven years old.

Familiar dread filled my heart, tightened my neck muscles, and sabotaged my peace. Hadn't we been through enough already? Now we had to deal with cancer? Why? I prayed.

I received no answer to "why?" So, I put on a stoic attitude, buried my emotions, ate all the junk food I could find, and lived with mounting acid reflux, taut muscles, and terse interactions with my family.

We consulted several doctors, including two kidney specialists who told us about three different options.

First, Martin could watch and wait. Prostate cancer grows slowly in most men. However, Martin was not like most men. Cancer cells could grow faster in him because of his immune-suppressed state.

Second, he could treat it with targeted radiation therapy. Don, Martin's eighty-eight-year-old father, had battled the dreaded disease with radiation, and it prolonged his life for a few years. Martin was only in his late fifties. We wanted more than a few years.

Besides, he had the kidney to consider. The specialists said targeted radiation should not affect the kidney—but there was no guarantee. Moreover, radiation didn't remove the cancer, which could come back years down the road. When the time came that Martin would need a new kidney, active cancer—even slow-growing cancer—could disqualify him from a second transplant.

The third possibility was for surgery, which put the organ at risk. Removing a prostate was a surgery that involved the renal system, the very system hooked up to the transplanted organ. Surgery could damage a stable transplant and induce kidney failure. If that happened, Martin would be back on dialysis and searching for a new donor.

Each solution had its drawback. None guaranteed a positive outcome. What should we do?

Past fears returned, fears I thought I had laid to rest, fears that God wanted a larger sacrifice of me than I wanted to give. The Lord didn't always make everything better. Both Martin, his sister Jean, and his father were proof. Martin's first wife died of breast cancer. Jean's husband, Rolf, died from liver cancer. And prostate cancer was taking the life of Martin's father.

God had asked for a tremendous sacrifice from all these family members. Why wouldn't He ask me to do the same? I didn't want to give that sacrifice. Just not wanting it wouldn't be enough. If it was God's will, it would happen. How would I find peace in the not-knowing stage? What should I do?

Giving up and doing nothing didn't feel right. As described earlier, I'm a fighter. Giving up meant surrender; it meant losing. There had to be something I could do to find peace. Should I write a thank-you note every day to my friends and associates? Gratitude helps us focus on our blessings. Should I spend more time ministering to others? Service lightens our own burdens. Should I attend the temple twice a week? Temple worship brings hope and peace. What should I do?

My answer remained elusive for a long, long time. One morning, I asked the same question I'd repeated often. "What more can I do?"

"Nothing more." The impression was distinct and puzzling and not what I'd expected. Do nothing? But "doing things" is what I do best. Baffled, I pondered the prompting and tried to comprehend what the Lord was telling me. I understood the message when I analyzed Christ's words to a group of Nephites and saw a distinct mirror to my life.

As the God Jehovah, Jesus gave the Israelites a law of performances. They had to sacrifice animals to help them remember the Savior's atoning sacrifice. It was something to do. That's what I wanted—something to do.

After Christ's death, though, He told the Nephites He would "accept none of [their] sacrifices and . . . burnt offerings" (3 Nephi 9:19). Instead, He said, "ye shall offer for a sacrifice unto me a broken heart and a contrite spirit" (3 Nephi 9:20).

That was the mirror that gave me my answer. God wants my heart and my spirit, not just my to-do list. Don't get me wrong. He wants a people who will keep covenants and commandments, who will serve Him, and who will build His kingdom. But going overboard is not the answer.

The sacrifice He required was for me to submit to Him. In the words of Neal A. Maxwell, "real, personal sacrifice never was placing an animal on the altar. Instead, it is a willingness to put the animal in us upon the altar and letting it be consumed!" ("Deny Yourselves of All Ungodliness," 68).

He wanted my heart, my life, my will.

Submitting to God is not always easy. In prayer after prayer, my cries ascended to Him for help to accept His will and to trust Him. With His help, I had success—sometimes. Frustration, anger, worry, and rebellion dominated too often. I kept trying. I kept praying. I kept adjusting my attitude. Bit by bit, peace descended on my soul, and remained only with the continued depth of my prayers.

Martin and I spent weeks praying to know which solution would be the best. He analyzed the information and weighed the options. Surgery appeared to be the one that would best protect both his life and his kidney.

On a cold Wednesday in January 2018—six years and one day after transplant—Martin returned to the Intermountain Medical Center in Murray, Utah.

This time it was me who fidgeted the hours away in the waiting room. This time it was me who sighed relief and prayed with gratitude when the doctor appeared with the message that Martin was doing well. This time it was me who awoke in the middle of the night in the hospital when my husband needed help.

His kidney had been sluggish all day after surgery. The massive amounts of IV fluid weren't being discharged. We guessed the lethargic organ resulted from the bowel prep from the previous day, the surgery, the pain meds, or all three. Martin had been alert and in good spirits all day. Nothing to worry about.

I stayed overnight the first day in case he needed anything. The makeshift bed was uncomfortable, and I'd tossed and turned. Whirring machines and sporadic inflating blood pressure cuffs filled the otherwise quiet room. Every two or three hours, a nurse's visit disturbed the quiet. They checked blood pressure, gave him medication, drew blood for early labs.

At four in the morning, the on-call doctor threw on the overhead lights and rushed into the room. The kidney had stopped working. Martin was in acute renal failure.

What? I shook my groggy head and tried to focus.

Two orderlies appeared before I could take it all in. They lifted the side rails to his bed and wheeled him out of the room.

In a daze, I scrambled out of the tangled blanket. No time to change out of my sweats. I gathered our clothes, my book, and my computer and stuffed them into a tote. Did I have everything? Yes. The gurney was moving down the hall with my husband on it. I darted after the bed. The men held the elevator door for me, and I crammed into the tight space.

My shoulders pinched high and tight. A knot flared across the back of my neck. Blood left my knuckles and fingers as I clenched the tote in one hand. Cold shaking fingers of my other hand clamped onto Martin's hand.

Questions tumbled over themselves, each competing for attention, each demanding answers I didn't have, each feeding the terror that won its place at the front of my brain. What did this mean? Why now, fourteen hours after surgery? It had to be serious, or they wouldn't whisk him away to ICU. Could they save the kidney? They had to save the kidney. They just had to. It was the deciding factor in the route Martin had chosen. He wanted to protect the organ. Now this? I prayed Martin would not be back on dialysis before noon.

I stared down at him without talking and refused to express my fears so they could they float on the air and fall on him. He had to have his own fiends running rampant inside his head. He didn't need mine too.

"It'll be all right," I said, my voice soft, desperate.

He squeezed my hand.

The elevator jolted to a stop, and the doors opened. I pushed out of the way and then followed behind the bed to the intensive care room.

The ICU doctor looked at Martin's vitals. A few minutes later, Martin's surgeon arrived, unshaven and wearing an outside coat. Someone must have awakened him in the middle of the night with the news one of his patients wasn't doing well. The two doctors consulted with each other and contacted the on-call kidney doctor. After a long discussion, they gave him some hydrocortisone and changed some of the IV fluids.

I didn't understand everything they did. The medical terms and how the changes would help Martin recover flew over my head. But I knew enough to realize that Martin didn't respond as soon as he should have. They made more adjustments, and we waited.

The room lightened. Dawn already? When had that happened? How long had I sat perched on the edge of the flat chair cushion next to my husband?

Bright daylight seeped between the cracks in the blinds. The nurse drew another vial of blood from Martin. Another test result came back. The treatment was working. Martin's kidney was waking up. Sixteen hours later they discharged him from ICU and returned him to the regular hospital floor. We went home the next day.

All went well for ten days.

Bleeding started. Don't worry, the doctors said. He should have some residual bleeding from surgery. It ebbed and flowed, but got worse. Martin's pain climbed and didn't recede.

"Michelle," he awoke me in the middle of the night a week later. "I think I have a fever."

"What time is it?" I staggered out of bed.

"After two in the morning."

Eyes half closed, I searched for the thermometer, not worried, eager to get back to sleep. Temperatures often rise in the night. But since fever was one indicator of a rejection episode, we always checked it when it climbed. If it got too high, we had to go to the ER.

Just like we'd always done, we would check it, debate a few minutes about whether it was high enough to go to the hospital. We'd decide it wasn't, go back to bed, and check it again in the morning. Just like we'd always done.

One hundred and two. It had never been that high in the night.

"We need to go to the ER, right now," I said, all sleepiness gone.

Martin shifted and caught a sharp breath. "It hurts." He panted and groaned, his face ashen. "I'm gonna throw up." He tried to stand and winced. I grabbed a needed bucket.

Fearful questions competed for my attention once again. What was happening? Was this a problem from the surgery? Was he rejecting the kidney? Why was he in so much pain?

I pulled the car out of the garage. Martin climbed in, and we were off. He grimaced and held his breath with every bump on the road. Once at the ER, the words high fever, recent surgery, and kidney transplant pushed Martin through the red tape at record speed. Before we knew it, they hooked him up to IV antibiotics, wheeled him out of the emergency room, and admitted him to the hospital floor. The kidney was fine, but he had a dangerous internal infection that could take his life if it didn't clear up.

Again, family members looked after my son, Dennis, the only child now at home. Again, we consulted with various doctors to find a solution. Again, the ward prayed for us.

Every morning, I got Dennis off to school and left for the hospital. I curled up on the window bench of Martin's room and watched. I watched him. I watched the sun creep over the Wasatch Mountains and fill the Salt Lake Valley with brightness. I watched the nurses come and go. I watched the traffic thicken with the coming light, remain steady during the day, and thicken in the afternoon, this time going the opposite direction. I watched the evening lights twinkle on one at a time. I watched the life flight helicopter leave and come back too many times. Leave and come back with another person, another tragedy, another sacrifice.

Sacrifice is part of everyone's life. Jesus Christ sacrificed His whole life, everything He had and was. God asks us to mirror the Savior, to sacrifice our lives too. Everyone's trials and offerings to God are different. What He asked of me differed from what he asked of Martin and will differ from what He asks anyone else. The Lord might ask someone to surrender personal health or become caretakers of someone with poor health. The sacrifice might involve the agony associated with a loved one rejecting the Gospel. It could target financial, emotional, or social difficulties.

Whatever it is, we know it will be unique and personal, sometimes designed by God and sometimes simply allowed by God, but always required by God.

We can rejoice knowing that He never asks us to make these sacrifices alone. Jesus Christ descended below all things so He could help us (D&C 121:8). President Lorenzo Snow said, "The sacrifices that are required of us are of that nature that no man or woman could make them, unless aided by a supernatural power" (*Teachings*, 179).

Even as I watched Martin suffer in pain, I witnessed the Lord strengthen my heart. He wrapped me in His arms, in a cocoon of love and safety. He gave me power to get up each day, comfort my children, near or far, and minister to my husband with peace.

In the end, the Lord did not ask for a larger sacrifice of me or Martin, for which I'm grateful. Seven days after the ER visit, Martin's fever left, the internal infection gone, and the kidney still healthy. He could go home and heal.

After Martin left the hospital, I can't say we could finally proceed with a comfortable, easy life of building God's kingdom. Submitting our will to Him takes a lifetime. Trials come and go, such as disease, pandemics, and the death of loved ones. Sacrifice is not a once-and-done kind of deal. Martin's health too, isn't a once-and-done kind of deal. There are things he has to do every single day in order to maintain the integrity of his transplant. The road we have to travel isn't always easy.

Sometimes, I wonder why God requires us to give so much. I try to remember that what He asks is not just an academic exercise, or merely a means to get us to lean on Him. The Prophet Joseph Smith taught, "a religion that does not require the sacrifice of all things never has the power sufficient to produce the faith necessary unto life and salvation" (Guide to the Scriptures, "Sacrifice").

Everything God does has a purpose. "'For I know the plans I have for you,' declares the Lord, 'plans to prosper you and not to harm you, plans to give you hope and a future'" (Jeremiah 29:11, NIV). He wants to help us thrive, grow, and return home to live with and become like our Heavenly Father. Everything He does is to help us. Everything.

CHAPTER 19

FINAL TESTIMONIES

"All things which have been given of God from the beginning of the world, unto man, are the typifying of him."

(2 Nephi 11:4)

Looking for Christ in all things is not a gimmick. It's a lifestyle. When we examine the mirrors of Jesus found in our everyday lives, we will be more prepared to see His hand when the big trials hit. As we search for Him day by day, we will come to know Him better, trust Him more, and love Him deeper. Our ability to follow Him and keep His commandments will increase.

In the middle of our trial, even before we determined that I would be the donor, I wrote this in my journal:

"I am coming to know God better as I think about all the analogies with Martin's kidney failure. I am overwhelmed at how much more I love God now than I did six months ago.

"Has kidney failure and this trial been easy? No. Do I like it? No. Do I want it gone? Yes. Do I wish it had never happened?

"To that, I cannot anymore answer yes. Would I trade what I've learned about God and how close I've grown to Him for the absence of this trial?

"No."

I am truly humbled and grateful for the things I learned about the Savior. To that end, I share my deepened testimony. Because of my many experiences of fear, pain, anxiety, stress, peace, love, and mercy:

- I know with much greater surety that our Heavenly Father and Jesus Christ live!
- I know they are mindful of each one of us.
- I know they love us.
- I know the power of the atonement of Jesus Christ is real.
- I know that we need the sacrifice of our Redeemer in order to live.
- I know that although Christ pled with the Father for another way, He stayed faithful to the end because of His love for us and for Heavenly Father.
- I know that because of our Lord and Savior we can return home, and we can become like God!

I know these things because I learned them more deeply through the trials of my faith during Martin's transplant. I pray that all of you will find mirrors of Christ in your lives every day that will bring you closer to Him.

MARTIN'S TESTIMONY

I feel truly blessed to be able to share my testimony. You have read many parts of our surgery and struggle and the miracles that have been poured on us. I feel very humbled.

I came close to death and realize that if I had lived a hundred years ago, I would have died. The power of the priesthood was made manifest in my life in many ways before, during, and after the surgery. I came out of surgery and had a really hard time waking up from the anesthesia—four hours of a hard time!

The nurse practitioner that I had been working with talked about a drug that counteracts the effects of narcotics and the anesthesia. It took four times the usual amount to reverse the effects to help me wake up. I remember coming to, then falling back onto a pillow and repeating the process. They would say, "Martin, Martin, wake up!"

I knew I was supposed to wake up, but I was so tired. I thought, "Why is it so important that I need to wake up now?" And they said, "Martin, breathe!" Though I heard their words, I still couldn't come out of the deep sleep.

My dad felt inspired to come and give me a blessing. I remember them putting their hands on me and giving me a blessing. I remember coming out of the fog that I had been in for four hours.

One of the most humbling times was the next morning. The nurse was kind of surprised that I wanted to get up and walk so soon after the surgery. She told me I could if I felt well enough. I remember standing at the edge of my bed and it hurt! I felt sick, but I wanted to go see Michelle. I got hooked up to the mobile IV pole, and the nurse walked with me thirty yards to Michelle's room.

It made me so sad because I was feeling better, in a lot of pain, but better—I could think again after being in a fog for so long. As I went into Michelle's room, I could see that she couldn't even sit up in bed. She was hurting so much. I walked over to the bed as close as I could, but the best thing we could do was hold hands. I felt really sad that someone would have to suffer like that for me.

After the surgery and after we had recovered, I knew that we had truly been blessed because of the miraculous experiences we had and because of the many individuals who did kind things for us.

I saw the growth of my children spiritually and emotionally. Dennis had special help from beyond the veil, and Katie's testimony grew, as you have read. Another member of our family received a blessing from the Lord that we had long fasted and prayed for, a blessing that was the result of this trying experience. My children can bear testimony with greater authenticity because they had to rely on the Lord during this ordeal.

All of my life is precious to me. All of it. The good times and the adversity. All of the things I experience give me an intimate knowledge of our Father in Heaven. Sometimes the trials give me keener insight into the mind and will of our Father in Heaven. "And this is life eternal, that they might know thee the only true God, and Jesus Christ, whom thou hast sent" (John 17:3).

Through this trial I came to know Christ in more intimate and profound ways. Whatever I suffered, I knew that He had experienced it before me. He knew how to succor me by sending angels all along the way. Michelle made the greatest Christlike sacrifice, but there were so many others, my father and mother, my brothers and sisters, ward members and friends, too many to count, all of them following the Savior's example of selfless sacrifice.

I want to bear you my witness that priesthood power is real. Our Father in Heaven loves each of us and blesses us according to our faith and according to our needs. Many times He will intercede and the blessings that come from the righteous exercise of the priesthood are real! Jesus Christ knows me; He loves me. In my time of peril, He was there.

I bear you my witness that Jesus Christ lives. This is His church here upon the earth restored by the Prophet Joseph Smith. I testify that our Father in Heaven and Christ love us intimately, and that they have blessed me and will bless all of us in personal and wonderful ways.

I bear you this witness in the name of Jesus Christ, Amen.

Questions for Group Discussion or Personal Reflection

Chapter 1: Mirrors of Jesus are everywhere. What experiences have you had in your life that mirror the Savior's?

Chapter 2: Prophets point us to Jesus Christ. When have you heeded a prophet's counsel and grown closer to the Savior?

Chapter 3: Jesus Christ is the master healer. What experiences have you had where He has healed you and helped you get back on the right track?

Chapter 4: Christ learned by the things He suffered. How have you grown and learned through your sufferings?

Chapter 5: The Savior faced rejection from those around him and felt forsaken by His Father right before He died. When have you felt forsaken by others? When have you felt Christ run to you when you were all alone?

Chapter 6: The Savior carries our burdens and sorrows, and He rejoices in our success and happy times. When have you felt Him carrying your burdens? When have you felt Him rejoice with you?

Chapter 7: The Lord's timing is not always the same as our timing. When has He delayed helping you or answering your prayers? When looking back on your experiences from the vantage point of the future, when have you found His timing to be better than your own?

Chapter 8: Jesus served others as well as received service from others. When have you found joy through serving others? When have you been blessed by receiving service?

Chapter 9: Without the Savior's sacrifice, we cannot live. When have you experienced the benefit of a sacrifice on your behalf, either large or small, that helped you survive and move forward in life?

Chapter 10: Jesus had to be both man and God to save us. How has knowing that Jesus Christ suffered and endured the difficulties of life given you strength?

Chapter 11: Jesus did not receive all knowledge and power at first but grew in wisdom and stature. When have you grown bit by bit with the Savior's help? What experiences in your life have prepared you for the things you need to do now?

Chapter 12: God's thoughts are higher than our thoughts. When have you relied on the Lord without understanding why, only to learn He was right?

Chapter 13: Jesus pled for another way yet submitted. When have you faced a difficult challenge and submitted?

Chapter 14: The Savior was strengthened by an angel. When have you been strengthened by an angel, either mortal or spiritual?

Chapter 15: Our Redeemer focused on the joy that would come because of His sacrifice. When have you focused on the end result to survive a hard time?

Chapter 16: Jesus heals us and answers our prayers. When have you been healed or had your prayers answered?

Chapter 17: The Savior endured to the end. When have you pushed forward to endure? How have you relied on God for help to endure?

Chapter 18: God requires our hearts as a sacrifice. When have you submitted your will to Him? What is He asking you to submit to now, and how can you find strength to do so?

Chapter 19: In Doctrine and Covenants 76, the Lord told Joseph Smith and Sidney Rigdon to record their testimonies of the things they saw and heard. Martin and Michelle shared their testimonies of Jesus Christ and how He was made manifest in their lives. What can you record about the power of Jesus Christ in your life?

WORKS CITED

Andersen, Neil L. "Repent . . . That I May Heal You," *Ensign* or *Liahona*, November 2009, 40–43.

Ballard, M. Russell. "Precious Gifts from God," *Ensign* or *Liahona*, May 2018, 9–11.

Bednar, David A. "Bear Up Their Burdens with Ease," *Ensign* or *Liahona*, May 2014, 87–90.

Bible Dictionary, "Grace." Salt Lake City: The Church of Jesus Christ of Latter-day Saints, Revised 2013.

Book of Mormon: Another Testament of Jesus Christ. Salt Lake City: The Church of Jesus Christ of Latter-day Saints, Revised 2013.

Children's Songbook. Salt Lake City: The Church of Jesus Christ of Latter-day Saints, 1989.

Christofferson, D. Todd. "Redemption," *Ensign* or *Liahona*, May 2013, 109–12.

Craig, Michelle D. "Divine Discontent," *Ensign* or *Liahona*, November 2018, 52–55.

Doctrine and Covenants. Salt Lake City: The Church of Jesus Christ of Latter-day Saints, Revised 2013.

"Donation After Life," *HRSA, organdonor.gov*, Reviewed September 2021, https://www.organdonor.gov/learn/process/donation-after-life.

Eyring, Henry B. "Always," *Ensign* or *Liahona*, October 1999, https://www.churchofjesuschrist.org/study/ensign/1999/10/always?lang=eng.

Guide to the Scriptures, "Sacrifice," scriptures.ChurchofJesus Christ.org, https://www.churchofjesuschrist.org/study/scriptures/gs/sacrifice?lang=eng.

Hales, Robert D. "Agency: Essential to the Plan of Life," *Ensign* or *Liahona*, November 2010, 24–27.

Holland, Jeffrey R. *Christ and the New Covenant: The Messianic Message of the Book of Mormon.* Salt Lake City: Deseret Book, 1997.

Holland, Jeffrey R. "The Ministry of Angels," *Ensign* or *Liahona*, November 2008, 29–31.

Holland, Jeffrey R. "None Were with Him," *Ensign* or *Liahona*, May 2009, 86–88.

Holy Bible: King James Version (KJV). Salt Lake City: The Church of Jesus Christ of Latter-day Saints, Revised 2013.

Holy Bible: New International Version (NIV). Grand Rapids, MI: Zondervan Publishing House, 1984.

Hunter, Howard W. "The Opening and Closing of Doors," *Ensign*, November 1987, 54–60.

Jones, Joy D. "An Especially Noble Calling," *Ensign* or *Liahona*, May 2020, 15–17.

Joseph Smith Papers, The. "Minutes and Discourse, 9 June 1842," 61, Salt Lake City: Church Historian's Press. josephsmithpapers. org/paper-summary/minutes-and-discourse-9-june-1842/1.

Lawrence, Larry R. "What Lack I Yet?" *Ensign* or *Liahona*, November 2015, 33–35.

Maxwell, Neal A. "Deny Yourselves of All Ungodliness," *Ensign*, May 1995, 66–68.

Maxwell, Neal A. "Swallowed Up in the Will of the Father," *Ensign*, November 1995, 22–24.

McKay, Kyle S. "The Immediate Goodness of God," *Ensign* or *Liahona*, May 2019, 105–7.

Monson, Thomas S. "We Never Walk Alone," *Ensign* or *Liahona*, November 2013, 121–24.

Monson, Thomas S. "What Have I Done for Someone Today?" *Ensign* or *Liahona*, November 2009, 84–87.

Nelson, Russell M. "Hear Him," *Ensign* or *Liahona*, May 2020, 88–92.

Nelson, Russell M. "His Mission and Ministry," *New Era*, December 1999, https://www.churchofjesuschrist.org/study/new-era/1999/12/his-mission-and-ministry?lang=eng.

Nelson, Russell M. "Jesus Christ–The Master Healer," *Ensign* or *Liahona*, November 2005, 85–88.

Nelson, Russell M. "Joy and Spiritual Survival," *Ensign* or *Liahona*, November 2016, 81–84.

Nelson, Russell M. "Perfection Pending," *Ensign* or *Liahona*, November 1995, 86–88.

Nelson, Russell M. "Personal Priesthood Responsibility," *Ensign* or *Liahona*, November 2003, 44–47.

Nelson, Russell M. "Revelation for the Church, Revelation for Our Lives," *Ensign* or *Liahona*, May 2018, 93–96.

Oaks, Dallin H. "Love and Law," *Ensign* or *Liahona*, November 2009, 26–29.

Online Etymology Dictionary, s.v. "succor," updated April 5, 2018, https://www.etymonline.com/word/succor#etymonline_v_22294.

Pearl of Great Price. Salt Lake City: The Church of Jesus Christ of Latter-day Saints, Revised 2013.

Perry, L. Tom. "The Gospel of Jesus Christ," *Ensign* or *Liahona*, May 2008, 44–46.

Rasband, Ronald, A. "By Divine Design," *Ensign* or *Liahona*, November 2017, 55–57.

Scott, Richard G. "Trust in the Lord," *Ensign* or *Liahona*, November 1995, 16–18.

Stokes, John B. "Consequences of Frequent Hemodialysis: Comparison to Conventional Hemodialysis and Transplantation." *Transactions of the American Clinical and Climatological Association* 122 (2011):124–36, www.ncbi.nlm.nih.gov/pmc/articles/PMC3116337/. Accessed September 29, 2022.

Smith, Joseph. *History of The Church of Jesus Christ of Latter-day Saints*. Edited by B. H. Roberts. 2nd ed. rev., vol. 5, Salt Lake City: The Church of Jesus Christ of Latter-day Saints, 1932–51.

Snow, Lorenzo. *Teachings of Presidents of the Church: Lorenzo Snow*, Salt Lake City: The Church of Jesus Christ of Latter-day Saints, 2012.

Uchtdorf, Dieter F. "Continue in Patience," *Ensign* or *Liahona*, May 2010, 56–59.

Uchtdorf, Dieter F. "Fourth Door, Last Door" *Ensign* or *Liahona*, November 2016, 15–18.

Uchtdorf, Dieter F. "Your Great Adventure," *Ensign* or *Liahona*, November 2019, 86–89.

ABOUT THE AUTHOR

Michelle Dennis Christensen is a kidney donor, an award-winning author, a speaker, an avid family historian, and a chocolate lover. She is passionate about shining a spotlight on the Savior to share His love and light with others. Michelle likes sharing gospel principles in an approachable, applicable manner and thinks that a Gospel Doctrine teacher is the best calling ever.

When in her early thirties, Michelle married Martin Christensen, a widower with four children, and she left her career to be their mother. She and Martin were blessed to have two children together, and Michelle is grateful that all six children call her "Mom." You can connect with her and view more photos at MichelleDennisChristensen.com.

Scan to visit

michelledennischristensen.com

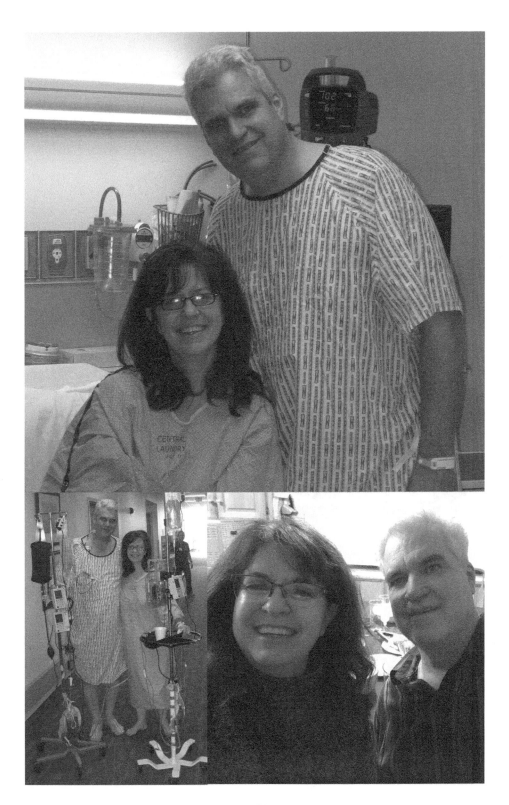